100 YEARS OF CHANGE

SPEED AND POWER

With grateful thanks to Frances Banfield, Ingrid
Cranfield, Lucinda Hawksley, Helen Johnson, Dave
Jones, Sonya Newland, Martin Noble and
Rana K. Williamson.

ISBN 0 75253 144 1

This edition published in 1999 by
PARRAGON
Queen Street House
4 Queen Street
Bath BA1 1HE

Created and produced for Parragon by
FOUNDRY DESIGN & PRODUCTION
a part of The Foundry Creative Media Company Ltd
Crabtree Hall, Crabtree Lane, Fulham,
London, SW6 6TY

100 YEARS OF CHANGE

SPEED AND POWER

Nigel Gross, Anthony Peacock, Kevin Raymond,
Tim Scott, Jon Sutherland and Alexander von Wegner

Foreword by

Richard Noble

Leader of ThrustSSC Project

Introduction by

David Tremayne

PARRAGON

Land speed records, 1898–1997

0   20   40   60   80   100   120   140   160   180   200   220   240   260   280   300   320   340   360   380

1898	JEANTAUD (CHASSELOUP-LAUBAT), ACHÈRES, 18 DECEMBER	63.15 km/h	39.24 mph	▶ p.100
1899	JENATZY (JENATZY), ACHÈRES, 17 JANUARY	66.65 km/h	41.42 mph	▶ p.100
1899	JEANTAUD (CHASSELOUP-LAUBAT), ACHÈRES, 17 JANUARY	70.31 km/h	43.69 mph	▶ p.100
1899	JENATZY (JENATZY), ACHÈRES, 27 JANUARY	80.33 km/h	49.92 mph	▶ p.100
1899	JEANTAUD (CHASSELOUP-LAUBAT), ACHÈRES, 4 MARCH	92.69 km/h	57.60 mph	▶ p.100
1899	JENATZY (JENATZY), ACHÈRES, 29 APRIL	105.87 km/h	65.79 mph	▶ p.100
1902	SERPOLLET (SERPOLLET), NICE, 13 APRIL	120.79 km/h	75.06 mph	▶ p.101
1902	MORS (VANDERBILT), ABLIS, 5 AUGUST	122.43 km/h	76.08 mph	▶ p.102
1902	MORS (FOURNIER), DOURDAN, 5 NOVEMBER	123.27 km/h	76.60 mph	▶ p.102
1902	MORS (AUGIÈRES), DOURDAN, 17 NOVEMBER	124.12 km/h	77.13 mph	▶ p.102
1903	GOBRON-BRILLIÉ (DURAY), OSTEND, 17 JULY	134.32 km/h	83.47 mph	▶ p.103
1903	GOBRON-BRILLIÉ (DURAY), DOURDAN, 5 NOVEMBER	136.35 km/h	84.73 mph	▶ p.103
1904	FORD (FORD), LAKE ST CLAIR, 12 JANUARY	147.01 km/h	91.37 mph	
1904	MERCEDES (VANDERBILT), DAYTONA, 27 JANUARY	148.51 km/h	92.30 mph	
1904	GOBRON-BRILLIÉ (RIGOLLY), NICE, 31 MARCH	152.50 km/h	94.78 mph	
1904	MERCEDES (DE CATERS), OSTEND, 25 MAY	156.47 km/h	97.25 mph	
1904	GOBRON-BRILLIÉ (RIGOLLY), OSTEND, 21 JULY	166.61 km/h	103.55 mph	
1904	DARRACQ (BARAS), OSTEND, 13 NOVEMBER	168.17 km/h	104.52 mph	
1905	NAPIER (MACDONALD), DAYTONA, 25 JANUARY	168.38 km/h	104.65 mph	
1905	DARRACQ (HEMERY), ARLES-SALON, 30 DECEMBER	176.42 km/h	109.65 mph	
1906	STANLEY (MARRIOTT), DAYTONA, 23 JANUARY	195.64 km/h	121.57 mph	▶ p.103
1909	BENZ (HEMERY), BROOKLANDS, 8 NOVEMBER	202.69 km/h	125.95 mph	▶ p.103
1910	BENZ (OLDFIELD), DAYTONA, 16 MARCH	211.26 km/h	131.275 mph	▶ p.103 (a)
1911	BENZ (BURMAN), DAYTONA, 23 APRIL	227.50 km/h	141.37 mph	▶ p.103 (a)
1914	BENZ (HORNSTED), BROOKLANDS 24 JUNE	199.67 km/h	124.10 mph	▶ p.104 (b)
1919	PACKARD (DE PALMA), DAYTONA, 17 FEBUARY	241.14 km/h	149.875 mph	(a)
1920	DUESENBERG (MILTON), DAYTONA, 27 APRIL	251.05 km/h	156.03 mph	(a)
1922	SUNBEAM (GUINNESS), BROOKLANDS, 17 MAY	215.24 km/h	133.75 mph	▶ p.104
1924	DELAGE (R.THOMAS), ARPAJON, 6 JULY	230.74 km/h	143.41 mph	
1924	FIAT (ELDRIDGE), ARPAJON, 12 JULY	234.93 km/h	146.01 mph	
1924	SUNBEAM (CAMPBELL), PENDINE 25 SEPTEMBER	235.17 km/h	146.16 mph	
1925	SUNBEAM (CAMPBELL), PENDINE, 21 JULY	242.57 km/h	150.76 mph	
1926	SUNBEAM (SEAGRAVE), SOUTHPORT 16 MARCH	245.15 km/h	152.33 mph	▶ p.104
1926	BABS (THOMAS), PENDINE, 27 APRIL	272.45 km/h	169.30 mph	▶ p.105
1926	BABS (THOMAS), PENDINE, 28 APRIL	275.22 km/h	171.02 mph	▶ p.105
1927	BLUEBIRD (CAMPBELL), PENDINE, 4 FEBUARY	281.439 km/h	174.883 mph	▶ p.106
1927	SUNBEAM (SEGRAVE), DAYTONA, 29 MARCH	327.95 km/h	203.792 mph	▶ p.104
1928	BLUEBIRD (CAMPBELL), DAYTONA, 19 FEBRUARY	333.054 km/h	206.956 mph	▶ p.106
1928	TRIPLEX (KEACH) DAYTONA, 22 APRIL	333.95 km/h	207.552 mph	
1929	GOLDEN ARROW (SEGRAVE), DAYTONA, 11 MARCH	372.39 km/h	231.446 mph	
1931	BLUEBIRD (CAMPBELL), DAYTONA, 5 FEBRUARY	395.95 km/h	246.09 mph	
1932	BLUEBIRD (CAMPBELL), DAYTONA, 24 FEBRUARY	408.63 km/h	253.97 mph	
1933	BLUEBIRD (CAMPBELL), DAYTONA, 22 FEBRUARY	438.469 km/h	272.46 mph	▶ p.106
1935	BLUEBIRD (CAMPBELL), DAYTONA, 7 MARCH	445.40 km/h	276.82 mph	▶ p.106
1935	BLUEBIRD (CAMPBELL), BONNEVILLE, 3 SEPTEMBER	484.606 km/h	301.129 mph	▶ p.106
1937	THUNDERBOLT (EYSTON), BONNEVILLE, 19 NOVEMBER	502.10 km/h	312.00 mph	▶ p.107
1938	THUNDERBOLT (EYSTON), BONNEVILLE, 27 AUGUST	556.01 km/h	345.50 mph	▶ p.107
1938	RAILTON (COBB), BONNEVILLE, 15 SEPTEMBER	563.57 km/h	350.20 mph	▶ p.107
1938	THUNDERBOLT (EYSTON), BONNEVILLE, 16 SEPTEMBER	575.32 km/h	357.50 mph	▶ p.107
1939	RAILTON (COBB), BONNEVILLE, 23 AUGUST	594.95 km/h	369.70 mph	▶ p.107
1947	RAILTON (COBB), BONNEVILLE, 16 SEPTEMBER	634.38 km/h	394.20 mph	▶ p.107
1963	SPIRIT OF AMERICA (BREEDLOVE), BONNEVILLE, 5 AUGUST	655.70 km/h	407.45 mph	▶ p.108 (c)
1964	BLUEBIRD (D. CAMPBELL), LAKE EYRE, 17 JULY	648.708 km/h	403.10 mph	▶ p.106 (d)
1964	WINGFOOT EXPRESS (GREEN), BONNEVILLE, 2 OCTOBER	664.96 km/h	413.20 mph	▶ p.108
1964	GREEN MONSTER (ARFONS), BONNEVILLE, 5 OCTOBER	698.46 km/h	434.02 mph	▶ p.108, 109
1964	SPIRIT OF AMERICA (BREEDLOVE), BONNEVILLE, 13 OCTOBER	754.31 km/h	468.72 mph	▶ p.108 (c)
1964	SPIRIT OF AMERICA (BREEDLOVE), BOONEVILLE, 15 OCTOBER	846.94 km/h	526.28 mph	▶ p.108 (c)
1964	GREEN MONSTER (ARFONS), BONNEVILLE, 27 OCTOBER	863.72 km/h	536.71 mph	▶ p.109
1965	SPIRIT OF AMERICA-SONIC 1 (BREEDLOVE), BONNEVILLE, 2 NOVEMBER	893.93 km/h	555.483 mph	▶ p.109, 110
1965	GREEN MONSTER (ARFONS), BONNEVILLE, 7 NOVEMBER	927.84 km/h	576.553 mph	▶ p.109
1965	GOLDENROD (SUMMERS), BONNEVILLE, 13 NOVEMBER	658.52 km/h	409.277 mph	(d)
1965	SPIRIT OF AMERICA-SONIC 1 (BREEDLOVE), BONNEVILLE, 15 NOVEMBER	966.54 km/h	600.601 mph	▶ p.109, 110
1970	THE BLUE FLAME (GABELICH), BONNEVILLE, 23 OCTOBER	1001.639 km/h	622.407 mph	▶ p.111
1983	THRUST 2 (NOBLE), BLACK ROCK DESERT, 4 OCTOBER	1019.44 km/h	633.468 mph	▶ p.113
1997	THRUSTSSC (GREEN), BLACK ROCK DESERT, 15 OCTOBER	1227.952 km/h	763.03518 mph	▶ p.113 (e)

420	440	460	480	500	520	540	560	580	600	620	640	660	680	700	720	740	760	780	MPH
▼	▼	▼	▼	▼	▼	▼	▼	▼	▼	▼	▼	▼	▼	▼	▼	▼	▼	▼	

Key

(a) Records not recognized by European authority.

(b) The first mandatory two-way run. The two-way run was introduced to allow fairer comparison between competing record-breaking claims. To be accepted, a record-breaking speed has to be calculated as the average of two runs, in both directions of the course, to eliminate factors such as gradient and wind.

(c) The first pure jet-propelled speeds, recognized by the motorcycle authority since the vehicle was a three-wheeler.

(d) Records achieved by wheel-driven vehicles. These had become a special category with the introduction of faster jet-propelled vehicles.

(e) The first record to break the sound barrier.

Order of information: year, maker/name of vehicle, driver, location, month/day.

Contents

Rocket-powered sledge
Sammy Miller's 'Oxygen' fuels his 'need for speed' 50

Sola Star
The hybrid future of transport? 51

Sunraycer
General Motors' solar-powered transcontinental racer 52

Truck racing
The only motor sport with a speed limit 53

3. GRAND PRIX MOTOR RACING 55

Paris – Rouen
The first ever horseless carriage race, July 1894 56

Nation shall compete against nation
The Gordon Bennett Races, 1900–05 57

The birth of Grand Prix
Circuit de la Sarthe, France, 1906 58

A quantum leap in technology
Mercedes and Auto Union between the wars, 1921–37 59

Mercedes W196
The most successful fuel-injected postwar car, 1954–55 60

The appliance of science
Cornering techniques in the 1960s 62

Peter Gethin at Monza
Fastest ever and narrowest winning margin Grand Prix, 1971 63

Lotus 79
Chapman's 'something for nothing' ground-effect car, 1978 65

Triumph of the 'yellow teapot'
Jabouille's victory in the Renault RS10, 1979 66

The Flying Finn's fastest ever qualifying lap
Keke Rosberg at the British Grand Prix, 1985 67

The century's fastest racetrack
The argument rages on … 69

'The Professor'
Alain Prost's record 51 Grand Prix wins 70

Ayrton Senna
Death of a superstar, May 1994 73

Scotland's Beatle-capped crusader
Jackie Stewart – safety-conscious Formula 1 ace 74

The most romantic name
Enzo Ferrari launches a legend 75

Team Lotus
The triumph and the tragedy 76

McLaren International
A reputation for immaculate preparation 77

Williams Grand Prix engineering
The sweet smell of success 79

Grand Prix Greats
The 10 fastest laps in Grand Prix history (since 1950) 80

4. INDY CAR RACING 85

Birth of the Brickyard
American motor sport is born, May 1911 86

'The only true sport'
Indy gets faster … and faster, 1925 87

'Super-sub'
Frank Lockhart's one-lap qualifying record, May 1926 88

'Just concentrate and go, go, go…'
Four-lap qualifying record, May 1990 89

'…like riding a bullet fired from a gun'
Luyendyk's 220 mph Indy Racing League lap, 1997 90

A. J. Foyt
Foyt – spelt 'F OYT', pronounced 'Indy' 91

Arie Luyendyk
The fastest man on tyres in Indianapolis 92

Il Leone roars
Nigel Mansell and his Lola-Chevrolet T9300 93

'Thrill of a lifetime'
Rick Mears – four-time Indy 500 winner 95

Bill Vukovich x 2
Indy's father-and-son dynasty 97

Foreword

I HAVE BEEN LOOKING FORWARD TO THIS BOOK, ALL ABOUT our fascination with performance and speed – and the power needed to achieve that speed. There is more to all this than just the well-known and simple calculation that speed varies in relation to the cube of the power provided. For instance, a current Formula 1 car requires around 750 bhp to achieve a speed in excess of 321.86 km/h (200 mph) – and our latest car, ThrustSSC, required 106,000 bhp to get to a peak speed of 1240.53 km/h (771 mph) and Mach 1.03. It is also important to remember that the kinetic energy increases with the square of the speed – and it is this often huge accumulated energy level that has to be dissipated to bring the vehicle to a safe halt. Of course the high-speed vehicle has to have the power to be fast – but it also has to be stable (to add power to an unstable vehicle is plain irresponsible) and to be braked: in short, it has to be safe.

There is another important factor: high power and unsilenced engines can generate huge noise levels – and unless happy with this, the local inhabitants will quickly bring any record-breaking attempt to a halt. So there is an important new social dimension.

There is something immensely basic and exciting about speed. I remember exceeding 64.36 km/h (40 mph) on a bicycle for the first time as a kid – and the thrill is very addictive. Having taken part in two successful world land speed attempts I am convinced that it is the most exciting thing you can do on the planet – and it's legal!

If you go right back to the birth of the motor car in 1898, the fastest thing on wheels at the time was undoubtedly the train, and even the bicycling record at 62.75 km/h (39 mph) was faster than the car! However, the huge public interest in the car and the social freedoms it brought ensured that it attracted considerable media attention and, consequently, it was subject to astonishing development. The importance of the early racetracks like Brooklands enabled the parallel development of the race car and the land speed record cars. The land speed record was in fact taken at Brooklands three times between 1909 and 1922. Thirty years later Grand Prix cars were hitting 321.86 km/h (200 mph) and the land speed record was a touch under 643.73 km/h

(400 mph), but that was on the Bonneville Salt Flats in the US. The urban Brooklands track had not been resurrected after the Second World War.

To build any of these record-breakers means that the design team and the driver have to break new ground – doing the same as the current holder is just not good enough – so innovation is a crucial ingredient to success. We did this with ThrustSSC – no one has ever built a 10-tonne twin-engined car with rear-wheel steer and active ride before! And with that innovation comes considerable additional risk, personal to the driver and private to the designer or design team. When you see the footage of John Cobb's, Donald Campbell's, or Craig Arfons's appalling deaths in water speed record boats, the risk and cost become absolutely unacceptable.

So why this fascination with speed? Well, there is undoubtedly the addiction, and of course the burning desire to do something better than anyone else and demonstrate it in a highly public manner. Anything that travels faster and enables you, for example, to achieve more work in 48 hours is seen as not only acceptable but also highly desirable. But there is the other side to the social acceptability. There was a time when Grand Prix cars were seen as important development vehicles for road cars, but it would be difficult to make that argument today. Today's road cars need to be smaller, cleaner, safer, more economic and more comfortable: there is no longer room for the outright performance.

Because of the huge cost of developing safe racetracks, the Grand Prix car's speed is severely restricted – a smart balancing act between car performance, spectacle and the cost of rebuilding the track to provide greater safety for the spectators. Not so long ago, turbojet-powered airliners made an appalling noise which was unacceptable both in terms of noise and fuel burn. Then we saw the switch to the quieter, more efficient turbofan engine and now airliner noise is only a distraction when you live at the wrong end of the runway. Frank Whittle saw all this in the 1950s when he came up with the turbofan design, but people did not listen then.

They are still not listening when they talk of the possibility of hypersonic space planes taking off from Heathrow or O'Hare airports. It took years for the public to accept limited Concorde flights, so how are those same people going to react to a 400-tonne, 250-decibel scramjet-powered monster belting westwards towards Windsor Castle along runway 27R at 643.73 km/h (400 mph)?

From now on, exploits in speed and power are going to be increasingly limited by social acceptance. When we ran ThrustSSC through the sound barrier, our research had suggested that there would be a slight sonic bang. There was – but only at the mid-point of the course. At the little town of Gerlach, just 19.31 km (12 miles) away, there was a monstrous great double bang, which shook windows, walls and upset the school's sprinkler system. The citizens of Gerlach took all this in their stride and were amazed by the novel experience – but it only takes a little imagination to recognize that there is a limit to how long they would accept that level of abuse.

In the past, land speed record attempts were carried out in remote deserts. Now the speeds are so high that there is only one good site in the world – the Black Rock Desert in Nevada. The Nevada population is growing and there must come a time when the citizens of Gerlach tell us enough is enough! After all, the 10-tonne ThrustSSC travelling out of control at Mach 1.02 could destroy the entire town. It could cover the 12 miles to Gerlach in under 60 seconds. There would be no time to get out of the way!

But the lure of speed and power still has that primitive attraction – manufacturers still charge more for their more powerful performance cars and there will always be the fascination with exotic Grand Prix engineering. There will always be that thrill of owning, travelling in or controlling the

ultimate machinery. There will always be the market.

But today the market dictates that the engineering challenge is to combine speed, power, stability – and social acceptance. And that opens up a huge new dimension. Like many, I am looking forward to the greater challenge with eager anticipation!

Richard Noble
Farnborough, January 1998

Introduction

Speed: it has always been such an emotive and evocative word. And for most of the twentieth century it has been a motivating factor that has inspired many to astonishing achievements, even though in the present age of caution and proscription, when moral guardians seek to protect people from themselves, it is more often than not frowned upon. The conquest of distance and time has been a fundamental factor in mankind's development these past 100 years.

Consider: in 1898, 80.46 km/h (50 mph) was believed to be well-nigh impossible. There were, indeed, those who believed that the human frame simply could not withstand the effects of such velocity. Travel was something that nobody undertook lightly, whether it was overland by horse or horsedrawn carriage, or overseas, when sailing ships took weeks or months to reach far-flung destinations.

Down the intervening decades the unceasing quest for speed has not only led mankind to the furthest corners of his own world with hitherto undreamed-of haste, opening up the planet, but has also allowed him to break free of its shackles. Speed has enabled him to traverse water rapidly, to emulate the birds and to fly. Today Concorde, beautiful enough to bring tears to the eyes of grown men, links Britain to America by flight lasting a mere three hours. Progress led mankind to venture not just into space, but to the very moon itself. And all within one incredible century.

Understanding and overcoming the forces unleashed by speed, no matter what the discipline or the environment, has given mankind better control over his environment. And harnessing such forces to his benefit has been one of the great challenges of the past 100 technological years.

Speed brought the aeroplane, the speedboat, the ocean liner, the motor car, the motorcycle, the high-speed train. Everywhere you look today in society, we reap the long-term legacy of those who pioneered it. Speed gets us where we want to go, sooner, more efficiently. It enhances our communication, our commerce, it is what makes the world go round. And it entertains us, when we watch cars, boats and motorcycles competing on the racetrack.

Life never stands still, and the quest for yet higher speeds is a pure endeavour that should be encouraged, for in daily life speed remains everything. Speed of communication; speed of response; speed of achievement. By nature, humans are not bred to stand still.

The killjoys regularly trot out the cliched line: speed kills. And surely it does, when applied injudiciously. Constraints and limitations are essential, in certain environments such as the public roads. But to the people who have sought the correct environment of the racetrack, the remote desert, the tranquil lake, the air – the car and boat racers, the test pilots whose brave exploits have led to benefits that have been passed down to ordinary air commuters, those who have sought ultimate speed records – it is the control of speed that has been so challenging. There is nothing whatsoever wrong with speed in these proper environments, correctly applied.

There is another component, more esoteric. And this is the inspiration provided by such speed-seekers. Many people lead sedentary lives, for it is easier to be a follower or a watcher than a doer. But consider the inspiration that pilots of, say, the Lockheed SR71 Blackbird strategic reconnaissance plane, can provide to future generations. Men capable of

Those who are unprepared to expose themselves to that chill feeling of fear and self-doubt that can precede even the most heroic deeds, before shrugging off such thoughts to venture forth and face and conquer the challenge, should be grateful to those who are, and salute exploits which over 100 years have helped to lay the very foundations for today's high-tech world, which so many take for granted.

This book is a celebration of such exploits, covering many realms of speed. Often it is a tale of courage against the odds in the quest for speed. But more than anything it is a story of commitment. Persistent, painstaking and unerring commitment.

David Tremayne

controlling a
vehicle on the very edge of its
performance ability, up to 107 km (67
miles) above the earth, when the temperature
of its skin reaches more than 715 °C (1320 °F).
Or flying it consistently and safely even though a mere
one degree change in its angle of flight can lead them 900 metres (3000 feet)
off trajectory – every minute.

Or men such as Andy Green, who coped with yaw angles that took ThrustSSC up to 15 metres (50 feet) off its course, yet kept his foot firmly to the floor during the trial runs that eventually led him to smash through the sound barrier on land and boost the speed record to a staggering 1220.86 km/h (763.035 mph). Sound role models. Those who have experienced at first hand holding any kind of powered vehicle in a controlled slide, who have successfully snatched a position from a rival on a racetrack or beaten the clock in search of a new record, will understand the intoxicating thrill of competing against oneself or against others. Or of competing against, and beating, the forces of nature. And anybody who has felt those forces doubled, trebled, quadrupled, who has been massaged by the vibration of a finely honed machine and kept it within their control even while pushing it to and sometimes beyond the edge, will appreciate that there are some things in life that are infinitely preferable to sitting in an armchair at home and simply watching others having fun.

Aviation

1

There are at least a dozen ways that the X-1 can kill you, so your concentration is total.

Chuck Yeager, first man through the sound barrier

Overleaf: the Gloster Meteor, the first British jet fighter (see page 24).

Top: the first successful flight of the Wright Flyer at Kittyhawk, North Carolina in December 1903.

Bottom: the Wright Flyer was constructed from wood and wire with a fabric skin, it also had an unusually light engine, enabling the Wright brothers to succeed where others had failed.

The Wright Flyer
The first controlled and sustained flight, December 1903

BEING ABLE TO FLY LIKE THE BIRDS HAD BEEN AN ASPIRATION OF MANKIND SINCE PRE-HISTORY, THOUGH until the Montgolfier brothers first ascended in a hot-air balloon in 1783 all attempts had resulted in ignominious failure, serious injury or death ... more often than not, all three.

While ballooning technology improved throughout the nineteenth century, along with significant progress in unpowered gliders, the ultimate goal of powered flight remained unattainable. The fact was that no matter how good the basic design might be, the engines available were simply too heavy. It was not until the dawn of the twentieth century that internal combustion engines finally offered the answer.

There were numerous attempts to be the first to achieve powered flight, and this honour fell to two American brothers, Wilbur and Orville Wright. The Wright brothers were bicycle designers and manufacturers by trade, but both had a passion for flying. It was their ability to build powerful and light combustion engines that was to be the secret of their success.

The Wright Flyer was a delicate structure of wood and wire covered with a fabric skin. A biplane in configuration, it had the unusual feature of having the vertical control surface, the fin, mounted at the rear while the rest of the 'tail' was mounted on a boom at the front of the aircraft. However, it was not the airframe of the Flyer that made the machine so special – it was the engine. The Wright Brothers had designed and built it themselves and while being very light for its day it also managed to produce an output of 12 hp. It was connected to two pusher-propellers, each 2.4 m (8 ft) in length, mounted at the rear of the pilot's seat by bicycle chain, the total weight being 340 kg (750 lb).

The Wrights chose a deserted area of beach on the North Carolina coast near a small town called Kittyhawk to make their attempts. The sea breezes would help with the take-off and the broad stretches of flat sand provided an ideal runway.

It was on 17 December 1903 that the Flyer finally made it into the air, the last day before the brothers would have had to abandon the attempt until the following year. The flight itself does not sound at all impressive today, lasting only 12 seconds, with a peak altitude of around head height and managing a top speed of 48 km/h (30 mph).

Within a few years numerous other aircraft had achieved far more than the Flyer ever did, and it was left to others to capitalize fully on the achievements of the Wright Brothers. However, no one will ever be able to take away the fact that they were first – quite an achievement for a pair of bicycle builders!

The Model XI Monoplane
First flight across the English Channel, July 1909

LOUIS BLÉRIOT WAS IN THE AUDIENCE THE DAY THAT THE WRIGHT BROTHERS DEMONSTRATED THEIR FLYER IN 1908. Blériot had started flying in 1907 and it did not take him long to become a major player in the early history of aviation.

Blériot's most famous aeroplane was the Model XI, a machine that was altogether more advanced and sophisticated than any that had gone before it. It also had the distinction of being one of the first practical machines actually to look vaguely like a modern aeroplane. The engine was mounted in the machine's nose, it had a tail at the back and a single wing ... a monoplane.

Significantly lighter than the Wright brothers' Flyer, at around 300 kg (660 lb), the Model XI also sported a far more powerful 25 hp engine that could propel the machine at the breathtaking speed of 75 km/h (47 mph)! It's easy to laugh at these kinds of speeds, but it must be remembered that a few die-hard doctors were still convinced that travelling at any speed greater than a horse's gallop would lead to madness or even death.

Blériot is remembered principally as the first man to fly successfully across the English Channel. He achieved this feat on 25 July 1909, setting off early on Sunday morning from Les Baraques in France. It took him 36 ½ minutes to travel the 37.6 km (23 ½ miles) to Northfall Meadow

Right: Louis Bleriot, designer of the Model XI.

Left: the Model XI monoplane, the most sophisticated aircraft of its time, became the first plane to cross the English Channel.

near Dover Castle in England. The landing was apparently rather heavy. Few complained, however, least of all Blériot himself, who successfully claimed £1000 in prize money from the *Daily Mail* newspaper for his achievement. The spot where he landed is commemorated to this day by a concrete silhouette set into the grass.

When talking about his trip Blériot admitted that he had not come by the most direct route and had even been lost for a short while until he had spotted the English coast. This slight problem was caused, he said, by strong winds.

The Model XI had the advantage of being comparatively easy to manufacture, and was therefore cheap. A number were purchased by the Royal Flying Corps, as the fledgling RAF was then known, and it was in just such a plane that the first aviator casualties of the First World War occurred in August 1914. A machine in the service of No.3 Squadron on its way to France went out of control and crashed, sadly killing both the pilot and his mechanic.

Earlier, another Model XI, this time flown by one Capitano Piazza of the Italian air force, was the first aeroplane to be used in war, when it made a reconnaissance flight in October 1911.

All in all, the Model XI was a remarkable invention, and one that perhaps more than any other finally convinced people that the aeroplane was a practical, as well as a wondrous, machine.

The Nieuport-Delage 29

First airspeed record after the First World War, February 1920

THE ADVANCES ACHIEVED IN AVIATION THROUGH THE FIRST WORLD WAR WERE ENORMOUS, the necessities of war being the impetus for technological advance, a story that was to be repeated more than once throughout the twentieth century. The last recognized record before the start of the war had been set in September 1913 by a Frenchman, Maurice Prévost, in a French-manufactured Deperdussin monoplane. The French had dominated airspeed records since 1909, a period which had seen the record broken no fewer than twenty times!

The French aviation industry continued to be a major player throughout the war itself, producing many notable machines, and the company of Nieuport-Delage was one of the foremost. Edouard Nieuport himself had held the record twice in 1911, and once the war was over was determined that France would maintain her position at the top of the speed league.

The aircraft that was to enable Nieuport to continue the string of French successes was the Nieuport 29 or Nieuport Hispano-Suiza. This machine had been designed as a successor to the model 28, a somewhat disappointing late-war design which had the distressing habit of losing its fabric covering in mid-flight! While most of Nieuport's previous machines had followed a process of slow evolution from the previous model, the 29 was completely new and as such was not immediately recognizable as a Nieuport. The single biggest departure from previous designs was the adoption of a liquid-cooled inline engine, manufactured by the Hispano-Suiza (literally Spain-Switzerland) company. This prodigious powerplant delivered 300 hp through eight cylinders. Coupled with the slim fuselage which an inline engine allowed, this gave the Model 29 a theoretical top speed approaching 240 km/h (150 mph), significantly faster than anything else flying at that time.

Although only a very early prototype flew before the end of the war, the Model 29 was an immediate success, being purchased by the Belgian, Italian, Swiss and Japanese air forces, as well as by the French themselves. Nieuport recognized the importance of publicity when it came to export sales and encouraged Sadi Lecointe, a famous aviator of his time, to use the machine in his attempts at the airspeed record.

The first of these attempts was made on 7 February 1920, and with no trouble at all Lecointe set a record of 275.22 km/h (171.05 mph). There then followed no fewer than six further records by Spad and Blériot aircraft as well as the Model 29 before the year was out, the final one being a speed of 313 km/h (194.53 mph) set by Lecointe on 12 December. Three further records were to be set by Lecointe and Nieuport, the final one reaching 374.95 km/h (233.03 mph) on 15 February 1923.

This remarkable run of French domination was soon to be ended by the Americans, and the French would be the world record-holders only one more time. The next decade would belong to the floatplanes of the Schneider Trophy.

Opposite: the French dominated the airspeed record from 1909 and throughout the First World War. Nieuport-Delage was one of the foremost aircraft manufacturers.

The Supermarine S6
First aircraft to exceed 350 mph, September 1929

FOR A BRIEF PERIOD AT THE END OF THE 1920S AND THE START OF THE 1930S AIRSPEED RECORDS WERE DOMINATED BY THE BRITISH, thanks to a series of magnificent floatplanes designed by Reginald Mitchell, the man who was later to design the Spitfire. These revolutionary planes were designed specifically to take part in the Schneider Trophy, an event so popular in its time that over 100,000 spectators turned up to watch.

The Schneider Trophy was the brainchild of Jacques Schneider, a pioneer French aviator who once held the world altitude balloon record. Tragically, he was later injured and could no longer participate in the sport he loved, though being wealthy he could indulge himself in the next best thing – sponsoring a race. Recognizing that floatplane design was lagging behind the rest of aviation in general he decided that his race would feature only this type of plane and so, in 1912, the Schneider Trophy was inaugurated.

The first of Mitchell's aircraft to make its mark in the Trophy was the S5, in 1927. This aircraft was, for its day, of very advanced construction, and if the bulky floats are ignored bore more than a passing resemblance to the Spitfire. It won the race with an average speed of 453.282 km/h (285 mph) over the course, an improvement of over 50 km/h (31 mph) over the previous contest.

Mitchell and his small team were not content to rest on their laurels, however, and set about refining the S5. A new propeller was added and the powerplant was now the Rolls-Royce RV12 delivering an impressive 1920 hp. The all-metal design was retained, as was the open cockpit, rather anachronistically for such a modern plane. Weighing in at 2381 kg (5249 lb), the plane was confidently expected to exceed 565 km/h (350 mph).

The 1929 competition was to be held on the Solent, the winners of the previous competition being the hosts for the next, and while the S6 was very much a civil aircraft the team to fly it was provided by the RAF, captained by Squadron Leader A.H. Orlebar.

The weather was kind on 12 September 1929, the day of the race, and conditions were more or less perfect. Despite gallant resistance by the Italian team in their Macchi-designed machines, the S6s were unbeatable. Flying Officer Waghorn had the honour of piloting the winning S6, shattering every race record and achieving a new absolute speed record into the bargain at 585.4 km/h (370 mph), although, as had occurred so many times, the record was not recognized as official. To rectify this problem Orlebar flew another S6 later in the day just off the Isle of Wight, achieving the slightly less impressive speed of 575.62 km/h (357.75 mph). This, however, was officially ratified and still comfortably set a new world record.

Britain had now won two Schneider Trophy races in succession. If they managed to win the next one they would win the Trophy outright.

The Supermarine S6, which ran away with the prize and the airspeed record at the Schneider Trophy competition in 1929.

The Supermarine S6B
First aircraft to exceed 400 mph, September 1931

SOME OF THE EVENTS THAT LED UP TO THIS ACHIEVEMENT have already been covered in the previous entry on breaking the 565 km/h (350 mph) barrier. The Supermarine S6 had been a magnificent achievement but still Mitchell believed that the basic design could be improved upon, just as the original S5 had been.

The new S6B, while obviously a development of the earlier plane, underwent an extensive overhaul. The existing Rolls-Royce engine was comprehensively modified to increase power output from the 1920 hp of the S6 to 2530 in the S6B and, while the overall dimensions remained unchanged at 9.14 m (30 ft) span and 8.79 m (28 ft 10 in) length, the overall weight was reduced from 2381 kg (5249 lb) to 2245 kg (4950 lb).

While Supermarine were busy developing the S6B, Europe was experiencing the worst economic slump in history – the Great Depression. Money was so tight that the British government announced that it would be unable to organize the 1931 Schneider Trophy for lack of funds, and for a while it looked as if Britain's chance of winning it outright had slipped away. It was only when Lady Houston intervened with a personal donation of £100,000, a phenomenal sum at the time, that the race could go ahead.

The timely and unexpected intervention of Lady Houston came as an unpleasant surprise to both the Italian and French teams. The French, who were hotly tipped to win, were forced to drop out when their new engine, specifically designed for the race, failed to live up to expectations. They were rapidly followed by the Italians. Both then requested that the race be rescheduled, a request which the British promptly refused.

With no competition, the last Schneider Trophy was something of an anticlimax, with Flight Lieutenant John Boothman flying solo at a winning speed of 547.31 km/h (340.08 mph). Nevertheless, in near-perfect flying conditions Flight Lieutenant Stainforth later that day set a new record speed of 634 km/h (388 mph), though sadly yet again it was not officially ratified.

Convinced that the S6B could do better, the Schneider team continued to practise and on 29 September prepared for a record attempt off the Isle of Wight. The pilot, again Flight Lieutenant Stainforth, managed to achieve a recognized speed of 654.9 km/h (407.02 mph) and an unofficial speed of just over 668 km/h (415 mph).

With no more Schneider Trophy and Britain in deep recession there were to be no more Supermarine floatplanes. The record stood until 1934 when the Italians and Germans started to vie for it.

The lessons learnt from the S series were not wasted, however. Mitchell started work on a land-based version of the S6B, which he hoped would one day be bought by the RAF to replace its ancient biplane fighters. Mitchell liked to call this plane the Shrew and was quite annoyed when the RAF, having purchased the new machine, insisted on changing its name. The name it chose was Spitfire!

The Gloster Meteor

The first of the jet fighters reaches 600 mph, November 1945

THE GLOSTER METEOR WAS THE FIRST BRITISH OPERATIONAL JET FIGHTER TO FLY WHEN IT TOOK TO THE AIR IN MARCH 1943, AND WAS A CONTEMPORARY OF THE FIRST AMERICAN JET, THE BELL AIRACOMET. The brainchild of Sir Frank Whittle, a pioneer in jet engines, the Meteor came to fruition in spite of government indifference through much of its development, and is as much a testament to Whittle's dogged determination as it is to his engineering skills.

It was only when information regarding the already advanced German jet programme came to light that significant resources were made available for the project. The Meteor was a comparatively simple straight-wing design powered by twin Welland jet engines, and in this first incarnation gave only a modest performance with a top speed just short of 800 km/h (500 mph). Some 16 machines entered service with the RAF and had some limited success in dealing with V1 flying bombs.

However, work was progressing on a Meteor powered by twin Rolls-Royce Derwent engines, each developing 907 kg (2000 lb) of thrust. This version, known as the Mark 3, went into volume production in early 1945 and immediately showed its superiority to normal piston-engine fighters, though sadly it never went head-to-head with the German Messerschmitt Me 262.

At the end of the Second World War production of the Meteor continued apace, both for the RAF and for export, the basic Mark 3 diversifying into various subtypes for night-fighting, reconnaissance and ground attack. With the demise of the Germans, the British had, for a time, an almost total monopoly on jet aviation and started to set a series of both official and unofficial airspeed records. The first of these was in October 1945 when an F4 variant attained a speed of 970.23 km/h (603 mph).

Unfortunately this was not recognized as official owing to a minor infringement of the myriad rules associated with such records. The following month another F4, piloted by Group Captain H. J. Wilson, took off from an aerodrome near Herne Bay in Kent. There were to be no mistakes this time and the Meteor duly performed, returning an accredited speed of 975.67 km/h (606.38 mph). The same pilot and plane again took to the air in the afternoon, setting another record at 983.42 km/h (611.2 mph).

Work continued on improving the Meteor and the following year two more records were set, both on the same day again. This time Group Captain Donaldson in his F4 managed a top speed of 1003.31 km/h (623.45 mph), though the breaking of the 1000 km/h barrier went largely unnoticed in a still firmly imperial-measuring Britain!

This was to be the last of the Meteor airspeed records, the Americans taking over the following year with their Shooting Star and Skystreak, though this in no way detracted from the Meteor's achievements ... the first of the jets!

The Gloster Meteor, the first British jet fighter, making its first flight during the Second World War.

The Bell X1

The sound barrier is broken for the first time, October 1947

AFTER THE SECOND WORLD WAR THE BRITISH AND AMERICANS were both competing to be the first to break the sound barrier. Sadly, at least for the British, their programme was cancelled in 1946 as the government thought it too dangerous for a man to travel so fast! This left the way open for the Americans and the remarkable Bell X1.

The X1 was powered by a single E6000-C4 rocket motor delivering an enormous, for the time, 2723 kg (6000 lb) of thrust. This kind of propulsion was needed as neither propellers nor the available jet engines could provide enough power. Unfortunately it also meant the X1 had to be released already airborne, as the rocket did not have the endurance to facilitate both taking off and landing, although this problem was soon overcome by converting a heavy bomber to do the carrying job.

Previous experience with near-Mach 1 speed had been alarming. The aircraft experienced increasing intense turbulence and unresponsive controls. Thanks to considerable help from German scientists and research acquired at the end of the war, it became apparent that the design of the wing was critical. This research, which was eventually to lead to swept-back flying surfaces, suggested that the thinner the wing the more stable at high speed it would be. As such, the X1 had a wing like a knife edge.

The first flight of the X1 took place on 19 January 1946. Although the engine was not used on this occasion the aerodynamics of the aircraft proved sound, particularly the 'Thin Wing', which some doubted had enough strength to withstand the rigours of flight. Following further exhaustive tests the first powered flight was made in December of that year, and again proved successful.

Throughout 1947 flights continued, edging ever closer to the sound barrier, until eventually, on 14 October 1947, Captain Charles 'Chuck' Yeager finally became the first man to fly faster than the speed of sound. His X1 reached Mach 1.015 or 1078 km/h (670 mph) at an altitude of 12,800 m (42,000 ft).

Once the barrier had been broken and its properties experienced, if not yet fully understood, progress accelerated. In all, six X1 planes were built, eventually achieving speeds of Mach 2.435 and an altitude record of 27,430 m (90,000 ft).

With the experience gained from the X1 programme the Americans attained a head start in high-speed flight that has still, arguably, not been closed. The X series of research aircraft eventually developed into the X15 planes, which as well as posting unofficial speed records in excess of Mach 6 also flew so high that the pilots were officially allowed to call themselves astronauts!

Left: the American Bell X1 – the first aircraft to break the sound barrier – piloted by Major Charles Yeager.

Overleaf: the North American F86 Sabre incorporated designs from captured German aircraft and was widely used by the United States Air Force from 1949.

The F86 Sabre

As American as apple pie, but slightly faster –
700 mph is broken, July 1953

IMMEDIATELY AFTER THE END OF THE SECOND WORLD WAR the Americans found themselves lagging some way behind the British in terms of jet-powered aviation. Obviously this was not a state of affairs that could be tolerated and they set about an intensive programme to develop jets of their own.

The earliest of these were little more than existing conventional airframes with a jet engine attached and were of generally disappointing performance. The Douglas Skystreak and the North American F86 Sabre were altogether more impressive machines. The F86 was originally conceived at the end of 1945 with traditional straight wings and experienced consequent handling problems at high speed. Captured German research on swept-back flying services then became available and the F86 was redesigned to incorporate them, resulting in a much more capable aircraft.

The first prototype flew on 1 October 1947 and exceeded the speed of sound in a dive on 26 April the following year. The type was immediately ordered into volume production for the USAF, the first operational machines being delivered from February 1949. Meanwhile a Sabre had already acquired the current world airspeed record, attaining 1079.61 km/h (670.98 mph) in September 1948. This marked the start of the Sabre's dominance of the airspeed record that was to last until 1953, with various machines setting no fewer than four different records during this time.

The Sabre arrived at a very fortuitous time for the USAF: a few short months after the first machines reached front-line service the Korean War started, a conflict in which the aerial duels between Sabres and Russian-built MiG 15s were to become legendary. The Sabre was the only aircraft in the UN's arsenal that even came close to matching the MiG's performance, and without it the outcome of the war might have been very different.

Owing in no small part to its usefulness in the Korean war the Sabre became an instant success, with literally thousands being constructed, both for service in the USAF and numerous export customers, including the RAF. In terms of speed records, however, the Sabre's finest hour came in July 1953. This flight was made by the D variant of the basic Sabre, equipped for the first time with a fully afterburning engine (simply the capacity to have raw aviation spirit injected into the exhaust stream to augment the power) and the necessary electronics to allow it to fight in all weathers. The new engine greatly increased the Sabre's speed and on the 16th of that month Lieutenant Colonel William Barnes piloted his F86D to a speed of 1151.64 km/h (715.75 mph).

This was to be the last speed record set by the Sabre. A British machine, the Hawker Hunter, was waiting impatiently in the wings and set a new record just weeks later. The Sabre, however, continued to enjoy a successful military career and to this day continues in service with many of the world's air forces – quite an achievement for an aircraft over 50 years old!

The Supermarine Swift
A British aircraft reaches 737 mph, September 1953

THE SWIFT WAS THE FIRST BRITISH AIRCRAFT TO HAVE BOTH SWEPT WINGS AND A TAIL, AND WAS DESIGNED AND BUILT BY THE SAME COMPANY THAT CREATED THE SPITFIRE. The Swift, however, was not destined to match its illustrious ancestor.

The first true prototype of the Swift took to the air on 23 August 1950 and was known as the type 535. These early test flights were reasonably favourable and the Air Ministry decided that the Swift would make a suitable back-up if the Hawker Hunter proved a disappointment. Thus, with the sudden outbreak of the Korean war, an order was placed for 100 Swifts. By now the aircraft was powered by two AJ65 Avon engines,

which on paper at least made the Swift a very powerful machine.

Unfortunately there was not time to redesign the airframe for either the new engines or the four 30 mm cannons that were fitted instead of the projected two. The new engines did not cause too much difficulty since they were smaller than the earlier Nenes. The extra guns, however, were to be the Swift's nemesis. To make room for them and for their increased ammunition load, the wing roots were extended, which made a lot more room but devastated the Swift's handling. Numerous improvised fixes for this problem were tried but in the end the only way round it was to insert a considerable amount of ballast in the nose of the aircraft, which obviously did nothing for its performance!

Despite all these problems Supermarine now produced a new version of the Swift with afterburning engines, known as the F3. This still had the same handling problems and it was not until yet another new variant, the F4, was built in May 1953 that the handling problems were finally solved with a new design of tail plane.

It was Lieutenant Commander Michael Lithgow, RN, flying an F4 Swift, who set a new airspeed record on 26 September 1953, when it flew at 1183.74 km/h (735 mph). This broke a record set by a Hawker Hunter just three weeks previously, and was itself to be broken in a matter of days by an American Douglas Skyray.

The first Swifts entered RAF service in February 1954. Unfortunately these were the early F1 variants, and were almost immediately grounded because of handling problems. As for the F4, only nine examples were built since it was discovered that the aircraft's afterburners could not be lit at high altitude – not a good feature for a fighter!

The Swift finally developed into the F5 variant, designed for low-level reconnaissance, and at last became a useful military plane. The aircraft's afterburning engines worked perfectly well at low altitude and survived in service until the early 1960s, even winning a NATO reconnaissance competition in 1959.

Apart from breaking the airspeed record, the Swift was at best a mediocre aircraft as far as the military was concerned, and has been totally overshadowed by its contemporary, the Hawker Hunter.

Built as a military plane, the Supermarine Swift went through numerous design changes before a workable aircraft was achieved in the F5.

The Douglas Skyrocket
The Mach 2 breakthrough, November 1953

THE DOUGLAS SKYROCKET, LIKE ITS NEAR-CONTEMPORARY the Bell X1, was a rocket plane rather than a jet and as such needed to be carried aloft by means other than its own power. This usually entailed being slung beneath a large bomber, only to be released at high altitude from where its own powerplant could take over. This inability to take off under its own steam prohibited the official recognition of any speed records; however, in terms of absolute speed records the Skyrocket was, for its time, a worldbeater.

It has its origins in Douglas's earlier Skystreak. This straight-winged design was conventionally powered by a single Allison turbojet and was itself a record-breaker, setting two new records in August 1947. While these records were officially recognized, they were very much overshadowed by the X1, which went supersonic in October of the same year.

The original X1 lacked the capacity to travel much faster than Mach 1.4 and the Royal Navy, recognizing the potential of the Skystreak, commissioned Douglas to redesign it with an all-rocket propulsion unit as a research aircraft. The power was provided by one Reaction Motors rocket engine developing nearly 2720 kg (6000 lb) of thrust. The aircraft also made use of swept wings, which thanks to research captured from the Germans at the end of the Second World War, allowed the plane a far higher degree of control at high speeds.

Because of its status as a research plane, only three Skyrockets were built, but for such a small number they had a remarkably productive career, by November 1953 having compiled no fewer than 237 flights.

During this time two absolute records were set, both for speed, at Mach 1.88, and altitude, at 25,300 m (83,235 ft). This was a considerable achievement since the Skyrocket's designers had never expected it to go faster than Mach 1.6. In spite of this, it was generally felt that if pushed to its extreme limits the Skyrocket might just be able to beat Mach 2. However, if such an attempt were to be made then it had to be made quickly since a newly revamped X1, the imaginatively named X1A, was poised to break this speed itself.

With the agreement of A. Scott Crossfield, the chief test pilot, Douglas set about preparing one of the Skyrockets for the attempt, making numerous small adjustments, which included covering the whole aircraft in a coat of wax to reduce drag. The attempt at the record was made on 20 November 1953 despite Crossfield's being sick with 'flu, such was his determination to exceed Mach 2 first! Released from a B29 Bomber the Skyrocket climbed to 21,500 m (72,000 ft) before going into a power dive where the dial registered the magical Mach 2.005.

This record was not to last long. A little over a month later it was surpassed by Chuck Yeager in the X1A, but nothing could take away the fact that it was Skyrocket that beat Mach 2 first!

The Mikoyan Ye66

Enter the Bear – Russia takes the airspeed record, October 1959

THE MIKOYAN GUREVICH (MIG) DESIGN BUREAU WAS ONE OF RUSSIA'S MOST SUCCESSFUL AIRCRAFT DESIGN TEAMS OF THE SECOND WORLD WAR, though for obvious reasons its work did not become so well known as aircraft designed by Western companies. With the advent of the Cold War, Russian aircraft design became shrouded in an almost impenetrable veil of secrecy that led the West to have an over-inflated opinion of its own superiority. Their first encounter with the MiG 15 aircraft in the skies of Korea soon shattered this illusion, however, and started an all-out arms race that has only recently come to an end.

Steady evolution from one model to the next typifies Russian design philosophy, and the Ye66 can trace its lineage back to the MiG 15 and beyond. The Ye66 itself was simply a modified and highly tuned version of the MiG 21, an operational fighter, which itself was an evolution of the MiG 19 and in turn of the MiG 17 and so on. Throughout the 1950s the main thrust of fighter design had been, without putting it too bluntly, to make them faster, and as such the MiG 21 was no slouch with a top speed of just over Mach 2.

Since the Second World War the Americans and British had monopolized official airspeed records, and the Russians, ever aware of the importance of propaganda, decided that this state of affairs had to change. To this end they set about constructing the Ye66. The modifications required to make this aircraft a record-breaker were fairly minor, thanks to the speed of the standard MiG 21. At the same time they also produced the Ye66b that was adapted to set altitude records. This was again a fairly straight adaptation of the basic MiG 21, this time with large rockets strapped to the underside!

The Russians made all the arrangements that an officially ratified record required and on 31 October 1959 Colonel Georgi Mosolov took off from a military airbase in Tyumenskaya and posted a speed of 2387.48 km/h (1483.83 mph), a new world record.

Obviously this state of affairs enraged the Americans, who were every bit as aware of the importance of propaganda as the Russians, and just six weeks later they took the record back with a speed of 2455.74 km/h (1525.95 mph). This was beyond the capabilities of the Ye66 or any other MiG 21 derivative. However, the Russians had far from given up their quest for records. Prompted by the American development of the B70 Valkyrie bomber, the Russians developed the MiG 25 interceptor, an aircraft capable of Mach 3, and from it developed the Ye166. Piloted by the same Colonel Mosolov, and from the same airbase, this aircraft posted a speed of 2681 km/h (1665.89 mph). It would take the Americans nearly three years to break this record!

The North American X15
Science fiction of the Sixties – Mach 5 and beyond, 1961

DESPITE NEVER having been ratified, the records set by the American X15 research aircraft have never even been approached, let alone beaten.

The X15 project originated in 1955 and was conceived as a logical progression of the X1 project (also covered in this book). Both the United States Army and Navy issued a requirement for three aircraft that could reach Mach 7 and an altitude of 80,500 m (264,000 ft). At the time, and indeed even today, these requirements are close to science fiction.

The North American aircraft company was given the contract and set about designing what many thought at the time was the impossible. To withstand the extremes of temperature that the aircraft would experience, the airframe would have to be constructed out of titanium, a notoriously difficult metal to work with, and stainless steel. These materials would have to be worked with the utmost care as the slightest imperfection would lead to localized turbulence and heat build-up that could well destroy the whole plane.

The only powerplant remotely capable of reaching such speeds was a rocket, and the X15 was therefore fitted with a single Thiokol XLR99-RM2 rocket developing 28,855 kg (57,000 lb) of thrust. Fitting such a motor would necessitate the use of another aircraft to carry the X15 aloft since it would have insufficient fuel to take off on its own. Fortunately an ideal platform for this task was available in the Air Force's B52 heavy bomber.

The first flight of the X15 took place on 8 June 1959, but without the Thiokol rocket, which was still undergoing final tests. Even allowing for the fact that these interim motors delivered only 15,000 kg (33,000 lb) of thrust, the X15 still managed Mach 2.3.

Tests and flights continued throughout the early 1960s, with record after record being successively broken, but never ratified, culminating in a speed of Mach 6.06 in December 1963, during which the surface temperature of the airframe was measured at 715.6 °C (1320 °F).

One of the three aircraft was damaged during landing and the North Americans took the opportunity to modify it in light of what they had learnt from earlier flights. This machine, now designated X15A2, made its first flight on 28 June 1964. It is interesting to note that, while this machine was routinely exceeding Mach 6, the official record was held by the Russian E166, which was only just capable of Mach 3!

As well as being amazingly fast the X15 could also reach staggering altitudes, peaking at just over 107 km (67 miles) high. This altitude is technically out of the earth's atmosphere!

The X15s were retired at the end of the 1960s having reached a top speed of Mach 6.72. The experience with hypersonic flight gained from the X15 project proved to be of immense value to the United States and to date nothing has even come close to the X15s' achievements.

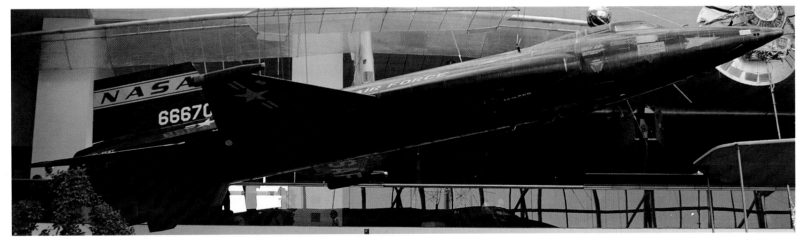

Powered by a rocket, the North American X15A was incredibly fast – exceeding Mach 6 – and could reach altitudes of 107 km (67 miles).

The B70 Valkyrie
The ride of the Valkyries – first of the big bombers, May 1964

HROUGHOUT THE 1950S THE STRATEGIC NUCLEAR deterrent of the world superpowers rested squarely on the shoulders of the air forces' heavy bomber fleets. In the case of the United States this meant the high subsonic B47 and B52 backed up by faster but smaller medium bombers, all of which were capable of carrying nuclear weapons.

The whole purpose of this aircraft was to penetrate hostile airspace, namely the Soviet Union, and drop bombs on it. Towards the end of the decade it became increasingly obvious that the existing designs of high-altitude bombers would not be capable of this for much longer, and that a faster replacement was desperately needed. This need was savagely underlined by the downing of a US Air Force's U2 spy plane over the Soviet Union in 1961 by an early SAM missile.

The US Air Force's answer to the growing problems of high-altitude penetration was to design a plane with more of everything: that plane was the B70 Valkyrie. The B70 had a top sustainable speed of Mach 3, considerably faster than any known fighter, making it almost impossible for any missile to intercept it.

To achieve this kind of performance required a radical departure from existing aircraft design practices. The B70 made use of early composite materials in its construction in order to increase the structure's strength, yet at the same time reduce its weight. The aircraft's power was supplied by no fewer than six General Electric J93 jet engines, each developing 14,062 kg (31,000 lb), making the B70 far and away the most powerful aircraft ever designed. These engines were married to a revolutionary airframe design that used twin tails, massive rectangular air intakes and a drooping nose. Delta wings were utilized to maximize high-altitude, straight-line performance. In front of the main wings was another pair of much smaller flying surfaces that performed the same function normally carried out by the aircraft's tail. This canard arrangement has since become common on the latest generation of high-tech military aircraft, owing to the control advantages it offers over traditional tail design.

The early test flights of the B70 were carried out in secret, but in early 1964 the air force went public with the project and revealed that it had in every way met its design requirements, easily reaching Mach 3.

Things were, however, not well with the B70 project. By 1964 missile technology had advanced and the B70 was beginning to look just as vulnerable as the planes it was supposed to be replacing, while being considerably more expensive. Not only that, but the first of the Navy's strategic ballistic missile submarines were now on line, making the whole idea of nuclear penetration bombing appear anachronistic. Additionally it was common knowledge in defence circles that the Soviet Union had designed its own high-speed interceptor to counter the B70, a machine that finally evolved into the MiG 25 Foxbat.

By late 1964 the government decided to cancel the whole project, the two extant models being used as high-speed test platforms. The B52, obsolescent in the late 1950s, still soldiers on today!

Left: *one of the original big bombers, the B70 was intended to penetrate Soviet airspace and was the most powerful aircraft built thus far.*

Opposite: *designed to solve the problems of high-altitude flight, the B70 Valkyrie was powered by six jet engines and had a revolutionary airframe.*

The TSR2
The greatest plane never built, January 1965

THE TSR2 (THE INITIALS STOOD FOR TACTICAL STRIKE AND Reconnaissance 2) can deservedly be called the greatest plane never built. Originally conceived as a replacement for the RAF's Canberra bomber, the design process started in 1956 with a protracted series of proposals and counter-proposals between aircraft manufacturers and the now-defunct Ministry of Supply. With the cost of developing modern aircraft soaring, it became necessary for companies to pool their resources in order to compete, and it was the merging of English Electric with Vickers to form the British Aircraft Corporation, or BAC, that secured the tender to develop TSR2. The process of tendering had been so protracted that this contract was not actually awarded until January 1960, with the first flight scheduled to be January 1963 and the plane to be in service by 1966.

The government of the day was keen that the management of the project proceed efficiently from now on and to this end looked at American methods of project management, implementing their results with TSR2 – with disastrous consequences! A nightmare of bureaucracy was born. At one meeting the chairman was concerned that there were too many people present and requested that they reconvene with only essential personnel present: more people turned up for the second meeting than had been at the first! At another the Ministry of Supply had a three-hour meeting to decide on the positioning of a single switch in the cockpit, only to have it pointed out to them by the chief test pilot Roly Faulk that the position fixed on made it impossible to reach!

Not surprisingly under the circumstances, the project slipped into delay and overspend and it was not until May 1964 that the first prototype was ready to commence trials. To complicate matters, there was an election looming, and, with the cancellation of the whole project a very real possibility, all the stops were pulled out to get the prototype airborne. Despite dire warnings from the engine manufacturers the flight was duly made on 27 September of that year. The flight itself was successful even though it was impossible to retract the undercarriage!

As time progressed the numerous problems with TSR2 were slowly ironed out, and from the mass of problems began to emerge an aircraft of quite glittering performance. The undercarriage problem was finally rectified after the 10th test flight, and on flight 14 the aircraft went supersonic for the first and only time, this being achieved with only one engine in afterburn.

Things, however, were not well with the project as a whole and on Budget Day, 6 April 1965, the project was scrapped without warning, to be replaced with F111s bought from the Americans. All tooling and drawings were destroyed, and parts scrapped with only two incomplete prototypes surviving.

In 1981 the government briefly looked at reinstating the TSR2 project, but with Tornado about to enter service this was soon quietly shelved, perhaps because a brief comparison revealed TSR2 to be still the superior machine 16 years down the line!

Above: After 14 test flights, the TSR2 finally exceeded the speed of sound, but figuratively speaking, the project never got off the ground.

Opposite: although it was commissioned in 1959, the TSR2 underwent a long and protracted phase of design and the first prototype was not revealed until 1964.

Concorde
The first supersonic passenger plane, March 1969

HE IDEA OF A COMMERCIAL AIRCRAFT THAT COULD CARRY OVER 100 PASSENGERS YET ALSO TRAVEL AT TWICE THE SPEED OF SOUND WAS BORN IN THE LATER 1950S, yet because of the great difficulties in constructing such a vehicle it was to be 1969 before the first one flew.

The British and French governments signed the agreement to undertake the project jointly in 1962. BAC in Britain and Aérospatiale in France were responsible for the design and construction. While aircraft are built in both countries, it is from a common store of parts built jointly by both companies.

Despite numerous problems, both technical and political, arising in no small part from spiralling costs, the project continued, while other rival projects fell by the wayside. The American Boeing 2707-300 was cancelled by a budget-conscious government, and the Soviet 'Concordski' floundered with technical problems.

It was to be the French Concorde that flew first, on 2 March 1969, followed by the British prototype a month later, and from the moment it first took to the air Concorde captured the imagination of the public. Few could deny the undoubted beauty of the aircraft, yet of all things it was the plane's drooping nose that seemed to cause most interest. A purely practical feature to increase pilot visibility when taking off and landing, it was affectionately dubbed the 'Droop Snoot' by the press.

Besides the refined aerodynamics and advanced delta wing, Concorde also sported a very impressive powerplant consisting of four Rolls-Royce SNECMA Olympus 593 Turbojets, each one producing 17260 kg (38,050 lb) of thrust, including full afterburning, a configuration that would still put many military jets to shame, and one which gave Concorde a top speed of fractionally over Mach 2.

Concorde taking off for its first transatlantic flight from Toulouse in 1976. It completed the journey in less than half the time of other commercial aircraft.

Test flights continued through 1969, the first supersonic flight occurring on 1 October of that same year. Things, however, still progressed slowly and it was not until 21 January 1976 that commercial flights started. On 24 May the first transatlantic flight arrived in Washington to be greeted by vast, cheering crowds and having completed the journey in under half the time of a normal airliner!

By this time, however, despite the brilliant technical achievement that Concorde undoubtedly was, all was not well. Considerable pressure was being exerted by environmentalists because of the noise and pollution that Concorde caused, and its undeniably high operating costs had cut projected sales of the aircraft from 72 down to 16. The Port Authority of New York banned Concorde from its airports because of the noise and it looked for a time that the whole project would again be axed. Fortunately, after a court case brought jointly by British Airways and Air France, this ban was overturned by the United States Supreme Court, and by the end of 1977 there were regular scheduled flights to New York – Concorde's future was secured.

After 25 years Concorde is still an amazing achievement and, with no firm plans for a successor, it looks set to remain the world's premier airliner for the foreseeable future.

The characteristic drooping nose of Concorde was designed simply to increase the pilot's visibility, but caused much interest when first revealed.

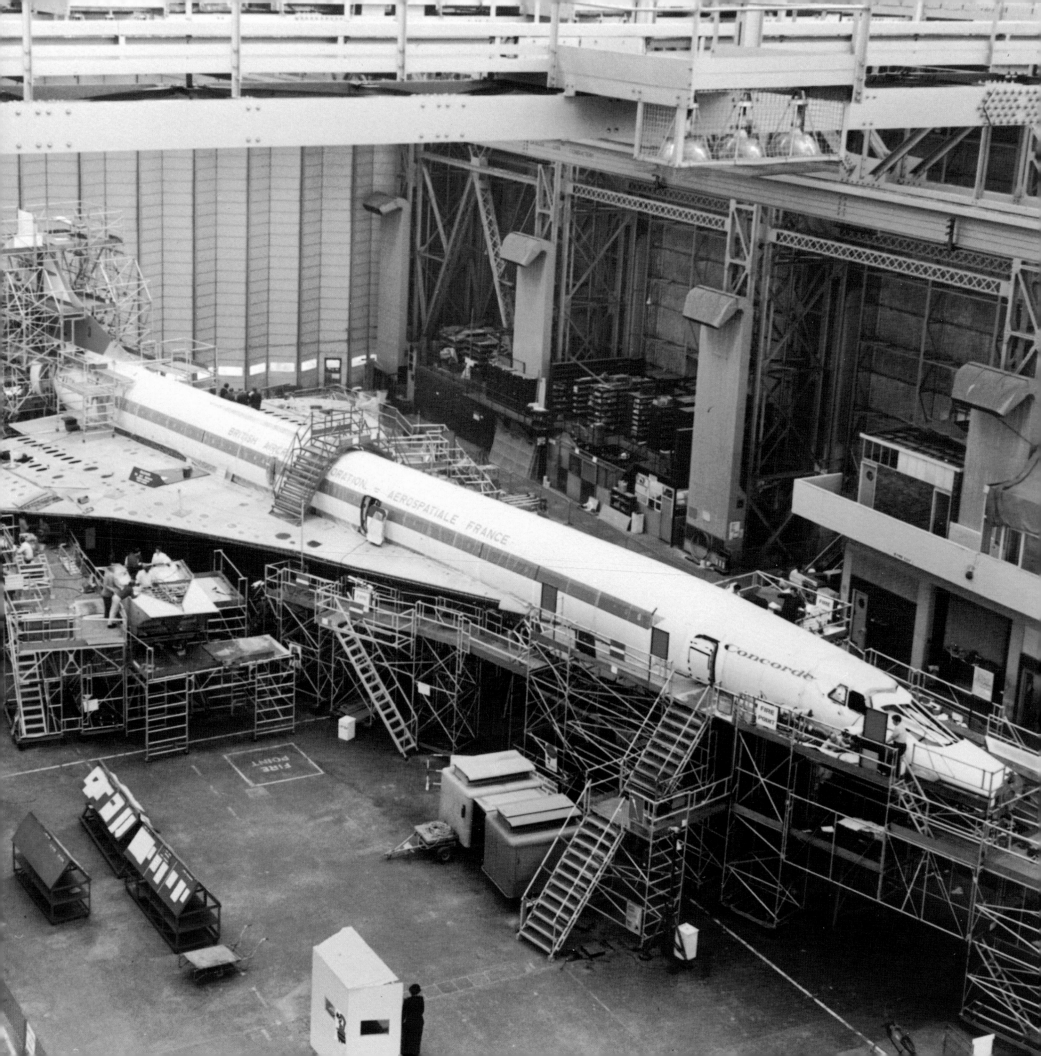

The SR71 Blackbird

Blackbird becomes the official airspeed record-holder, July 1976

LTHOUGH IT IS COMMONLY ACCEPTED THAT THE NORTH American X15 rocketplane achieved speeds in excess of Mach 6, the holder of the official record is the Lockheed SR71 Blackbird, and viewed from any perspective the Blackbird is a superlative machine.

Designed specifically for strategic reconnaissance duties from the outset, it had to be able not only to reach deep into the USSR but also fly high enough and fast enough to avoid interception. Altitude alone had been shown to be no defence when Gary Powers was shot down by a Soviet missile in 1961 when flying the SR71's predecessor through Soviet airspace.

To meet the requirements of both high speed and long range, the SR71 had to be large in order to carry the fuel necessary for such long round trips, consequently the powerplant had to be large. Large powerplants consume more fuel ... and so it can go on.

In the end the SR71 was a masterpiece of innovative design. Conceived and built in the utmost secrecy in the early 1960s, a prototype was revealed in 1964, and the first planes became operational in 1966. Because of its high top speed, reportedly approaching 3700 km/h (2300 mph), the design incorporated several novel features. All the planes were painted with a special black paint to help dissipate the immense amount of heat simply caused by friction with the air in the atmosphere. Additionally, some joints had to be constructed to allow expansion when the plane heated up, such that they had a tendency to leak when standing on the runway!

To meet its remit of strategic reconnaissance, the SR71 was also packed with high-technology equipment and was able to photograph accurately 259,000 sq. km (100,000 sq. miles) of terrain in one hour.

It was an SR71 that was the first true aircraft to break through the 3200 km/h (2000 mph) barrier, the X15 having been unable to take off under its own power. On 27 July 1976 one of them flew around a 1000 km (621 mile) circuit at an average speed of 3367.221 km/h (2092 mph) and 3529.56 km/h (2193 mph) in a straight-line dash. Not content with this, the same plane also set a new altitude record for sustained horizontal flight of 25,929 m (85,069 ft).

For an aircraft that was shrouded in secrecy for much of its operational life, and of which only 27 were ever produced, the SR71 has achieved great success, not to mention fame. There can be few people who have not seen photographs of this rather menacing plane, which is rather an interesting thought, given that the SR71 was designed specifically to be a secret spy plane!

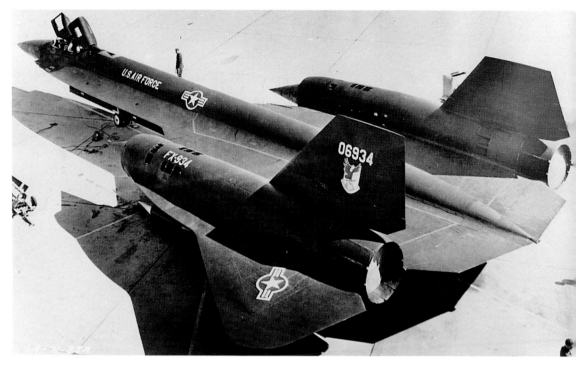

Above: *the Lockheed SR21s featured the very latest in hi-tech equipment, and broke both the airspeed and altitude records.*

Opposite: *twenty-five years on from Concorde's first flight, the aircraft is still the pinnacle of commercial aviation achievement.*

TUDOR LACENE P.L. TUDOR
LOGLIFT loaders
DAF FINA RACING TEAM
DAF FINA RACING TEAM
TOTAL TUDOR TOTAL
AMICALE DES
DEA
RWTÜV
Tiger Racing Team Dehnhardt
WFZ WFZ WFZ
ESSO CARD
ESSO
ESSO CARD
KNORR BREMSE
1
TUDOR
Continental
CEPSA
Diesel Star
MAN-Originalteile
SAF SK Axles Worldwide SAF
Team IRU Mobil
Mobil Delvac 1
TUDOR
2
IRU
Continental
CEPSA
DKV
EURO SERVICE
Ebers

Extraordinary Vehicles 2

Pushing a rocket car to its limit on acceleration is a real good kick. It kinda keeps me going, you know?

Sammy Miller, rocket dragster pilot

Dragster racing
Piling on the pressure – Sammy Miller endures 13G

SAMMY MILLER, BORN IN TEXAS, CAN QUITE RIGHTLY CLAIM TO BE ADDICTED TO TRAVELLING QUICKLY – very quickly. If he had a motto, it would be 'need for speed'.

Dragster racing originated in America in the 1950s. The idea behind a drag race is extremely simple – to go as fast as possible in the least possible time. So there are none of the complicated rules that surround the more conventional forms of racing: it is merely a question of go!

There are two fundamental principles of physics that restrict rapid forward motion, namely drag and friction. Drag comes from the physical resistance that a vehicle puts up against the air. Ultimately, very little can be done to avoid it. In order to make a car cleave the air quicker, you have to reduce the frontal area to a bare minimum, hence the reason that most fast projectiles are dart-shaped.

Dragsters have very small narrow noses to achieve this. The two brick-like front wheels are one of the biggest causes of drag in racing cars. To combat this, dragsters have front wheels which look similar to those fitted on a bicycle, although the thought of speeds of 380 km/h (200 mph) and being transmitted through them is admittedly scary.

Yet if you reduce the size of all the wheels, then you will naturally sacrifice traction, as the larger the contact patch is between tyre and road, the more of the engine's power you can transmit to the road. To compensate for the lack of grip at the front, dragsters have enormous tyres at the back. But this then creates greater friction between road and car, so what would somebody who wanted to travel really quickly in a dragster do about that? The answer is to dispense with wheels entirely. In his amazing record attempt, Sammy Miller made use of a 'funny car' dragster, which has skis instead of wheels. This lessens friction to an extent where absolutely staggering speeds are possible.

To be specific: 621.63 km/h (386.26 mph). For that is the speed that Sammy Miller obtained in November 1994 in his Mustang RFC dragster. No dragster pilot (for such they are called) has been quicker since. To illustrate the effects of that speed, Miller's car was wired with extensive telemetry allowing onlookers to dissect every moment of the journey.

The transition from 0 to 96 km/h (60 mph) was achieved in 0.21 sec, and from 0 to160 km/h (100 mph) in an incredible 0.35 sec. An eighth of a mile was covered in 1.606 sec, by which time the vehicle was travelling at 513 km/h (319 mph), and 0.4 km ($^1/_4$ mile) was achieved in 3.58 sec. To put this into its proper context: in one second the dragster accelerated from rest to 463 km/h (288 mph), exerting an excruciating 13G upon the pilot. A Formula 1 driver might experience 5G at the absolute limit. Normally the level of G force which Miller experienced would be harmful, but he was equipped with a pressure suit similiar to those worn by fighter pilots, to help him withstand it.

Fujiyama
The fastest steel rollercoaster in the world

SPEED IS RELATIVE. THE FERRARI F50 WOULD APPEAR PEDESTRIAN IN COMPARISON WITH THE PIONEER 10 SPACE PROBE, which started its journey travelling at about 51,682 km/h (32,114 mph). In the world of cars, 138 km/h (86 mph) is considered slow. After all, the top speed of a Lada Samara 1.1 is 140 km/h (87 mph). But when you are doing that speed in a rollercoaster, it takes on a whole new complexion (as does your face).

The fastest steel rollercoaster in the world is called Fujiyama, and it is in the Fujikyu Highland Park in Japan. And yes, it will transport you up to an utterly sick-making 138 km/h (86 mph). Through swoops, bends, loops

Above: Fujiyama currently holds the speed record for a steel rollercoaster, travelling at up to 138 km/h (86 mph).

Overleaf: the European Championship truck-racing circuit (see page 53).

and corkscrews, there is apparently nothing quite like it. Even the highly acclaimed Steel Phantom rollercoaster in Kennywood Amusement Park, West Mifflin, Pennsylvania, USA, has a design speed of only 128 km/h (80 mph), and this is a renowned 'coaster which drops 58 m (190 ft) into a natural ravine.

'It's simply amazing,' said Jon, an American student who had just emerged safely from Fujiyama, having unbuckled the (thankfully large and efficient-looking) safety cage. 'There's really nothing quite like it; you can feel your stomach turning around inside your body. It's like an addiction; afterwards you can't wait to go up again.' While not many people would claim to be actually addicted, it is easy to imagine the thrill that Fujiyama would impart. After all, it comes from a country that gave us sake, the Honda NSX and hara kiri. The Japanese like to enjoy themselves; for example they have the largest nightclub in the world, naturally in Tokyo.

Fujiyama supplanted Japan's previous record-breaking steel rollercoaster, which is called the Tojoko Land Loop Coaster, in Hyogo. Opened on 4 August 1979, it was not the longest or the fastest, but it certainly was the tallest, reaching a maximum height of 59.96 m (196 ft).

The tallest steel rollercoaster in the world at present is the appropriately named Desperado in Nevada, USA, which drops from a height of 63.7 m (209 ft). To put that into perspective, the Statue of Liberty is about 80 m (262 ft) high. But even then, Desperado can manage 'only' 127 km/h (79 mph) flat out.

Closer to home, the tallest rollercoaster in Europe is the Pepsi Max Big One in Blackpool. Big it certainly is, with a drop of 61.3 m (201 ft); enough to make Nelson's Column look small at a piffling 44.5 m (146 ft). But what about speed? Well, once again, even the 'Big One' has to concede second best to Japan's finest, running at a maximum of 128 km/h (80 mph).

So Fujiyama is truly king of the 'coasters. But wait, there is one device which is yet more tortuous. It is a machine called Dragon Khan at Port Aventura, Salou, Spain. In this rollercoaster, riders are turned upside-down eight times during the 1269.8 m (4166 ft)-long ride. How pleasant!

Competition is great in rollercoaster records, and longer, steeper and more hair-raising rides are always being planned.

Land yachts
Fast … and environmentally friendly

N THESE DAYS OF ENVIRONMENTAL AWARENESS, ANY FORM OF ECOLOGICALLY SOUND TRANSPORT IS BOUND TO BE SMILED UPON. The problem, however, is that most of the means of transport that genuinely do not pollute the environment tend to be of very little practical application.

Consider the land yacht. In its simplest forms it is just a plank affixed to wheels with a large movable spinnaker sail, allowing the pilot (or should that be captain?) to capture the wind wherever it might be blowing from. Just like its seafaring counterpart, the land yacht has to be carefully balanced and stabilized, which often results in perilous angles of lean for its occupant. The land yacht runs on four wheels; it is not uncommon for two of them to be cocked into the air at any given time. To compensate for this the pilot must lean back as far as possible in order to counterbalance the lean with his own bodyweight. This is naturally quite dangerous, so pilots are affixed to the main mast via a complex harness. It is also absolutely necessary to wear a helmet, as serious injuries to people can result from falling out and being dragged along the ground.

The sport originated in California in the early 1970s and soon caught on, being comparatively cheap and affording many thrills. In England it is practised above all in Cornwall, where the wide expanses of open beaches, coupled with quite strong winds for a lot of the year, have rendered the sport very popular. It is also popular on the flat beaches of Normandy and Brittany in northern France, which provide the correct climatic and geographical features. In fact, the world speed record for a land yacht powered solely by wind is held by a Frenchman, Bertrand Lambert, who achieved a remarkable 151.51 km/h (94.14 mph).

Above: *the land yacht world speed record is held by Bertrand Lambert, who sailed his craft at over 150 km/h.*

Opposite: *land yacht racing began in California in the early 1970s, and is popular in coastal areas where beaches provide perfect runs and the sea-winds offer the required power.*

Life in the fast lane
Kenworth JT is the fastest truck on earth

I N A RECENT SURVEY HELD BY THE AA, IT EMERGED THAT AMONG THE MAJOR PET HATES OF THE BRITISH MOTORIST WERE LORRIES that (illegally) hog the outside lane on motorways. The frustration is easy to understand, as by law lorries registered in the UK are fitted with speed limiters which are fixed at 90 km/h (56 mph).

But what if the lorries were unrestricted? A spokesman for DAF said that the modern generation of lorries were easily capable of speeds of more than 128 km/h (80 mph), depending on the load being pulled. After all, specialist racing lorries developed by Mercedes are able to reach speeds of over 217 km/h (135 mph) in unrestricted form, and the maximum speed ever attained by a development Mercedes turbo diesel racing truck is 247.4 km/h (153.7 mph) in 1997.

As impressive as that may sound, that is by no means the world's fastest lorry. Not by a long chalk. The claimant to that honour is a mighty Kenworth JT truck in America, which reached a speed of 375.23 km/h (233.16 mph) in 1994. Naturally this was no ordinary lorry, although it was based on a production chassis which, with a bit of imagination, could be said to resemble vaguely its more modest cousin. Kenworth is one of the biggest truck manufacturers in the USA, although the company was not officially involved in this venture.

Out went the standard V10 diesel block, and in came an ex-military rocket motor. To keep weight down, the lorry was extensively rebodied, with lighter plastic panels replacing the pressed steel of the cab. The lorry also wore tyres that were especially commissioned from Goodyear. To stop

Bob Motz set the truck racing speed record at 336 km/h (209 mph) in 1994, and has remained unbeaten since this time.

the vehicle, two huge parachutes were made, which were kept in a pocket on the roof. A lever inside the cab then activated them, and the truck would then coast to a halt. At least that was the theory, as the truck itself had no brakes, other than a single emergency pair. In the event of things going horribly wrong, the driver had woefully inadequate protection, consisting of a light steel roll cage and little else.

Bob Motz, driver of the lorry, said that his intention was to set a record which was slightly unusual. The phenomenon of drag-racing jet trucks has since caught on in the States, where only last year an attempt to beat Motz's record was staged. It failed, having reached a maximum speed of 'only' 336 km/h (209 mph). So Bob Motz remains the fastest truckie on earth, having reached 160 km/h (100 mph) from 0 in 2.9 sec – while driving a truck! Zero to 96 km/h (60 mph) was reached in 0.96 sec.

One of Steven Spielberg's early films was called *Duel*. It concerned a lorry purportedly vested with supernatural powers. As the victim of the story flees down a mountain road with the speedometer of his car pointing at 177 km/h (110mph) he wails, 'I don't believe it – how can he go so fast?'

It just goes to show that sometimes the truth really is stranger than fiction.

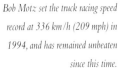

Mean Streak rollercoaster
The ultimate instrument of torture

IT WOULD INTEREST ANYBODY WITH A VENDETTA AGAINST their digestive system to know that the aptly named Mean Streak rollercoaster is one mean, stomach-churning piece of machinery. It is located in Cedar Park, Sandusky, Ohio, and it is the fastest all-wooden rollercoaster in the world. It's a slightly frightening thought that all that stands between you and certain, unpleasant death is an elaborate construction of what appear to be oversized matchsticks, but the 'coaster's owners, Cedar Park Amusements, say that the seven-year-old rollercoaster designed by Curtis Summers is safer than houses.

So breathe deeply. Count to 10. Relax. Here we go ... maximum speed on the Mean Streak is 105 km/h (65 mph) – that's 16 km/h (10 mph) quicker than the speed at which you can legally drive your car in the state of Ohio. It shares this maximum with the Texas Giant sick-maker in Arlington (should that be pronounced Hurlington?), Texas. This is certainly not as quick as the more modern steel rollercoasters, which attain speeds of over 128 km/h (80 mph) without much problem, but it is quick enough for a construction which initially looks about as safe as a one-legged man on a unicycle.

Furthermore, just to prolong the agony, Mean Streak has the longest circuit of any other wooden rollercoaster, at 1432 m (1566 yds). The records do not stop there, as Mean Streak is also the highest all-wooden rollercoaster in the world, its maximum height being a vertiginous 42 m (46 yds). The sadist responsible for designing this instrument of torture also incorporated the longest drop of any wooden rollercoaster, at a truly repulsive 40 m (43.7 yds). Assuming that you maintain a fairly constant 105 km/h (65 mph) during the descent, the total time taken would be a fraction over four seconds.

Cedar Park, a Mecca for rollercoaster lovers, is also home to Magnum XL-200, which was recently voted by *Inside Track*, an American magazine devoted to rollercoasters, as the 'awesomest' ride in the USA. Mean Streak doesn't get a look into the top 20, but interestingly enough, Texas Giant in Six Flags over Texas Amusement Park comes second in the survey – not bad for an all-wooden rollercoaster which never enjoyed the technological benefits of its steel brethren. In 1992, Texas Giant enjoyed the distinction of being voted 'Coaster of the Year' by the Inside Track readership.

It doesn't matter to the aficionados that Texas Giant has only the speed and not the length or drop of Mean Streak. Statistics have little to do with how a rollercoaster feels; it is an inexplicable, seat-of-the-pants sixth sense which dictates whether the feeling is there or not. Texas Giant, with its astonishing all-wood construction, is probably the Ferrari 250 GTO of the rollercoaster world: impractical, overtaken by modern design, but still astonishingly fast and great to travel in.

The Mean Streak is the fastest rollercoaster constructed entirely from wood, it is also the longest, making for a stomach-churning ride.

More than a hobby
Leonid Lipinski's model planes

BOEING 767 IS A MODERN, SPACIOUS AND COMFORTABLE aeroplane. Sitting comfortably in its metal and plastic cocoon, you will typically cruise at a speed of about 850 km/h (528 mph), maintaining an altitude of about 14,000 m (45,930 ft). At that speed and altitude, the outside temperature will be in the region of -75°C. Yet safely ensconced in the comfortable Boeing's interior, you have no impression of the forces that the elements are exerting upon the plane, thanks to its sheer size.

Smaller planes fly slower and lower, as their structures cannot withstand the stresses that high speeds necessarily cause. One man, however, set out to contradict that logic. A Russian engineer from Irkutsk, Leonid Lipinski, had been fascinated by flight from an early age, which led him to consider a career as a pilot. Sadly, he could not afford the cost of the training, so channelled his energy into building and flying model aeroplanes.

Initially, Leonid's model planes were just a hobby, but later he began to take it more seriously and consider ways in which he could achieve something lasting out of his hobby. In particular, in March 1971, he set about the task of building a model aeroplane which would be the fastest in the world, and approached it with typical dedication.

A model aeroplane of this sort would naturally need to be flown on control lines, as otherwise the very high speed would cause it to spiral instantly out of control. With control lines, a modicum of direction can be imposed upon the speeding plane.

Leonid achieved his dream on a bitterly cold 4 December 1971, nine months after embarking on the project. There was a slight tail wind as his aeroplane took off – perfect conditions for an assault on the record. His attempt two weeks previously had had to be curtailed, as the aeroplane developed a problem.

This time, though, things went perfectly, and the plane (which was made of reinforced plastic) reached a maximum speed of 395.64 km/h (245.84 mph). Remarkably, his record has remained unbeaten for 27 years, despite several attempts. The secretary of the British Model Aeroplane Association said:

'It's certainly a remarkable achievement. Everybody thinks that mucking about with model aeroplanes is just a little hobby, but there are some people who take it incredibly seriously indeed. I don't really know how the Russian man did it, but I wouldn't like to try and break his record myself. I've no doubt that somebody will, though, because development of model planes happens at the same pace as the real things. It's very surprising the record has lasted that long'.

Only time will tell. Meanwhile, Leonid Lipinski is a remarkable testament to what can be achieved with comparatively modest resources if you have an all-consuming passion. Let us hope that his record remains unbeaten for another 27 years.

Right: *Leonid Lipinski's interest in model aeroplanes led him to try and build the ultimate plane – the fastest in the world.*

Opposite and left: *the external pressures exerted on aircraft mean that smaller model planes must be carefully contructed if they are to weather the elements.*

Rocket-powered sledge
Sammy Miller's 'Oxygen' fuels his 'need for speed'

MAN WILL GO TO GREAT EXTREMES IN THE PURSUIT OF SPEED. Even to the extent of building ridiculous devices, which are more than vaguely absurd, just to prove a point. This has been the case throughout history, as the many examples of ludicrous seventeenth-century 'flying machines' patently demonstrate.

One such strange machine is the rocket-powered sledge. The sledge is one of the oldest forms of transport known to mankind, but the famed drag-racing record-breaker Sammy Miller put a somewhat strange slant on the whole theme. More specifically, he created a sledge propelled by two large rockets, and called his creation 'Oxygen'. The record for a rocket-powered sledge had not been established clearly before, so this was one superlative that Miller could be confident of making his mark on.

Ever the consummate showman, Miller staged his record-breaking run on the frozen Lake George in New York, after undertaking several tests to ensure that the ice was sufficiently thick throughout the whole length of the run to support the rocket sledge. It would have been more than a little embarrassing, after all, if his pride and joy had sunk before the eyes of the crowd of spectators who had turned up to watch the well-publicized event.

As it was, everything went entirely according to plan, and he roared his way to a magnificent 397.9 km/h (247.3 mph) on 15 February 1981, on a day where the ambient temperature was -8 °C. Interestingly, it was said that he could have gone even faster, possibly even cracking the 480 km/h (300 mph) barrier, but the confines of the lake would have made such an attempt too dangerous. It is important to note that the sledge was not fitted with rails at all, which meant that the whole attempt called for great precision on the part of the driver. One false move could have resulted in an irretrievable spin, with potentially disastrous results. It was just as well that Sammy Miller was no stranger to travelling quickly on ice.

Of all speed records ever attempted, perhaps this one was of the least practical use but that was certainly not the point for Sammy Miller, who wished to be the fastest man on the planet by whatever means possible. The majority of speed records are undertaken by highly technical groups, often with major corporate backing, but Sammy Miller did it more or less as a privateer for his own personal satisfaction.

Nobody has yet tried to better his record, but if they did, no doubt Sammy would respond, such is his 'need for speed', as the Americans say. In fact, being the holder of numerous records, including that for drag-racing rocket cars, one wonders exactly what he will think of next ... the world's fastest rocket-propelled shopping trolley, perhaps?

Sola Star
The hybrid future of transport?

UNLIKE MANY RECORD-BREAKING ATTEMPTS, THE SPEED record for a car powered by both solar and battery power is one that has an eminently practical application.

Bob Lutz, Chief Executive of Chrysler, said in 1990:

'It is certain that the concept of the automobile as we know it will be radically altered within a shorter space of time than the general public think. We are taking great steps to develop new forms of transport which do not depend on conventionally perceived power sources ... the hybrid solar/electric car is an option that we have been looking at for some time now, so that when the need for change comes, we will be in a well-placed position to react to it'.

In fact, most of the technology is in place to make hybrid vehicles which rely on a combination of solar and electrical power. The greater challenge is to persuade the market that this is a viable option.

Most record-breaking attempts which are to do with so-called 'alternative' power sources are officially sponsored by manufacturers, the rationale being that the lessons learnt will provide valuable feedback for future projects. This is not just an idle boast: Honda is rightly renowned for its VTEC variable-valve timing system which maximizes power yet aids fuel economy. Only a few years ago this was a development project on a concept car – now the system is fully mass-produced.

The Star Micronics Sola Star reached 135 km/h (83.9 mph) on 5 January 1991 at Richmond Royal Australian Air Force Base in New South Wales. It incorporated several of the features seen first on the General Motors Sunraycer, which set a speed of 78.39 km/h (48.71 mph) using solar power alone during 1988.

The main feature that the vehicles had in common was the regenerative braking system, which harnesses the wheels' motion to charge the battery during braking and descent. In theory at least, this comes close to answering the question that scientists have been asking for years: how to create a system of perpetual motion.

Outwardly, the Sola Star has the same form as the Sunraycer for maximum aerodynamic efficiency, although it incorporated a larger solar deck, but with a smaller number of cells. Initially, the vehicle got under way powered exclusively by the solar panels, then the stack of six batteries kicked in at about 48 km (30 miles) to move the car towards its top speed.

The most spooky thing of all is the fact that, bar a faint humming from the battery, the car ran at 135 km/h (83.9 mph) in near-total silence. The driver of the car was Australian Manfred Hermann, who had worked closely with the Star Micronics team in order to understand how to get the best out of the car. If it did nothing else, then hopefully it showed some of the doubting Thomases of the automotive world that a combination of solar and electrical power is indeed a valid option to power cars of the future – at high speed.

The Sola Star is aerodynamic in shape and is powered by a combination of solar cells and batteries which activate at 48 km (30 miles).

Sunraycer
General Motors' solar-powered transcontinental racer

THERE IS A FAMOUS ITALIAN SONNET BY PETRARCH WHOSE OPENING LINE IS 'PON MI 'OVE IL SOLE', ROUGHLY TRANSLATED AS 'PUT ME WHERE THE SUN IS'. Good advice, believe it or not, for General Motors, the largest car manufacturer in the world, whose 'Sunraycer' solar car achieved the solar land speed record of 78.39 km/h (48.71 mph) at Mesa, Arizona, USA, on 24 June 1988. No doubt it helps that Arizona – popularly known as Grand Canyon State – averages 0 cm of rainfall over the summer months and that temperatures can reach up to 54°C (130 °F) in August, but it is still a remarkable achievement.

those used on satellites such as the AUSSAT communication satellite for Australia. Each cell measures 2 by 6 cm (0.78 by 2.36 in), and is of about the same thickness as a credit card. Although the intensity of the sun's rays and ambient temperature affected the output, the car typically ran at 150 volts, providing about 1000 watts of peak electrical power at noon.

All this high technology is in stark contrast to the tyres on which the vehicle runs: they are 43 by 2.54 cm (17 in by 1 in) Moultons, more commonly seen on bicycles … .

Yet it was not just power output that determined the maximum speed. A lot of trouble was taken to ensure that weight was kept down to the minimum possible – for example, by using a special lightweight aluminium chassis. Aerodynamics would also play an important part in determining maximum speed. The shape of the car was partially designed by an advanced computer program called VSAERO developed by NASA. The result was a teardrop-shaped design which measured the lowest drag coefficient ever recorded for a road vehicle. In fact it was so slippery that a number of fins had to be placed on the car to ensure overall stability, particularly in crosswinds. A particularly clever feature was incorporated into the braking system which allowed the car essentially to 'freewheel' and use engine resistance to slow the car down. Via a flywheel this recharged the battery, hence the name 'regenerative braking system'.

It was hard work, but worth it for pilot Molly Brennen. When the car rolled to a regenerative halt, she was hot, but certainly not bothered.

The combination of the Sunraycer's lightweight aluminium chassis and its teardrop shape resulted in the lowest drag co-efficient ever recorded.

Described by GM as a 'solar-powered transcontinental racer', the vehicle was 6 m (20 ft) long by 2 m (6.5 ft) wide, with an all-up gross weight of 248 kg (547 lb). The majority of that was taken up by the 68 batteries, each producing 25 ampere-hours of energy.

This energy was accumulated via large solar panels on the 'car's' back, enabling it to accelerate to 40mph from rest in 20 seconds. Yes, that is incredibly slow, but it's not bad when you consider that it comes out of nothing. In any case the 'Sunraycer' has a back-up battery system which enables it to continue to heady speeds of 96 km/h (60 mph) plus.

The solar panels themselves (consisting of 7200 individual cells) were built by the Hughes Aircraft Company, to the same specification as

Truck racing
The only motor sport with a speed limit

IKE MOST VAGUELY ECCENTRIC THINGS, TRUCK RACING ORIGINATED IN THE UNITED STATES ABOUT 20 YEARS AGO, WITH RACING AROUND SHORT UNBANKED OVALS SUCH AS MILWAUKEE'S MILE.

But the history of European truck racing begins in 1984, with a race at Donington. This was the first international truck race in Europe run along properly RAC-sanctioned lines. Previously, regulations had been a bit hit and miss: basically, armed with any truck, you could turn up and race. With the formation of the BTRA (British Truck Racing Association) in 1984 all that changed. Drivers had to hold racing licences and trucks had to be fitted with compulsory safety equipment.

To raise the profile of the sport, the 1994 Donington race included celebrity drivers Martin Brundle (driving a Renault truck, not his regular F1 Tyrrell!) and motorcycle champion Barry Sheene, driving a DAF.

Nonetheless, the race was won by Italian Tullio Ghislotti, who drove over from Italy in his Volvo, unhitched his trailer, put in a roll cage and promptly won the event!

The modern European Truck Championship is a far cry from those tentative early days and is now almost as high-tech as Formula 1. The best championship to compare it to is the British Touring Car Championship. Like BTCC cars, the racing trucks resemble their road-going counterparts in outward appearance only. Engine size and weight distribution can be freely modified, subject to certain restrictions. The cab of a modern racing truck is a cross between a Formula 1 cockpit and a Boeing 747 flight deck, including racing seats and, most incongruously of all, a tiny sports steering wheel. The trucks are lighter than they seem, as all the teams try to shed weight wherever possible. The net result is an acceleration time of about 9.3 seconds from 0 to 160 km/h (100mph)!

Truck racing is the only form of motorsport with a speed limit: 160 km/h (100 mph). Unrestricted, the trucks could probably crack 225 km/h (140 mph). The limit makes racing much more exciting, as races are won or lost under cornering, acceleration or braking. Despite these leviathans' size, they are renowned for truly combative racing, with the sideways antics of drivers such as Jokke Kallio ('the Keke Rosberg of truck racing') adding to the spectacle.

Contrary to popular belief, the sport is very safe; accidents are more likely to result in major damage to the track than to drivers. A major rule change in 1994 split the trucks into two categories (essentially works and privateer) and limited engine capacity of the Class 1 trucks to 12 litres (2.64

gal). Previously, trucks had been running 18 litre (3.96 gal) V10 turbo diesels, capable of producing about 1800 brake horsepower!

The European Championship (nine rounds in 11 countries) is very popular, with meetings in Finland, Spain, Czech Republic and, best attended of all, Germany. It may not be the most subtle or economical form of racing, but in terms of spectacle it cannot be beaten. Just ask Mercedes driver Steve Parrish, winner of five European Championships to date.

Steve Parrish leading the European Championship, one of the most popular meets for truck-racing fanatics.

Grand Prix
3
Motor Racing

I am not designed to be second or third. I am designed to win.

Ayrton Senna, three-time World Champion

Paris – Rouen

The first ever horseless carriage race, July 1894

ODAY, RALLYING AND RACING ARE EASILY DISTINGUISHED: RACING MAINLY TAKES PLACE ON CLOSED CIRCUITS WITH TARMAC SURFACES, WHEREAS RALLYING IS A COMPETITION FROM A TO B, held in special stages on all kinds of roads and surfaces. But when the French paper *Le Petit Journal* announced the Concours des Voitures sans Chevaux (a 'test for horseless carriages') for 22 July 1894, this separation between rallies and races did not yet exist. Predominantly on loose road surfaces, the competitors drove from Paris to Rouen and back – so this would have been both a 'horseless carriage race' and a 'horseless carriage rally'.

The event of 1894 was not meant to be a speed contest. Rather, it was a 128 km (80-mile) reliability test and we have to remember that the automobile still had to establish itself as a serious alternative to traditional means of transport, so a reliability test seemed to be the ideal competition. The problem in 1894, however, was that most competitors turned the event into a race. The quickest car was Count de Dion's steam-powered device, which averaged 18.63 km/h (11.58 mph). This rather modest figure was quite remarkable, though, bearing in mind that the very first car was patented only on 29 January 1886 in Germany.

Count de Dion did not, however, win the Concours because the rules said that a driver had to have a mechanic with him – and de Dion drove on his own. Hence, Peugeot driver Lemaitre received the honours.

Technically, a trend had been started. Of the eight steam-powered cars at the start, four broke down, but all 13 of the petrol-powered cars finished. This was the beginning of the combustion engine's triumphal march.

If – for all the reasons stated above – the Paris-Rouen is not regarded as the world's maiden motor race, the event dated 11–13 June 1895 certainly is. Again, the start and finish of this first official motor race was in Paris, but the distance to Bordeaux and back added up to 1178 km (732 miles). And again, the quickest on the road was not the winner. Emile Levassor finished within 48 hr 48 min – almost six hours ahead of the second-placed Rigoulot. But neither the winning Panhard nor the Peugeot won any prize for they were two-seaters and only four-seaters were eligible.

Although Levassor's average of 24 km/h (15 mph) was hardly any quicker than Count de Dion's performance a year earlier, sheer speed should not be regarded as the main aim in those early days. Racing was still an adventure, but it was only the first step in the many adventures that were to come.

Overleaf: Ayrton Senna in action for McLaren (see page 77).

The appliance of science
Cornering techniques in the 1960s

I T IS DIFFICULT TO IDENTIFY THE DIFFERENCES BETWEEN A SLOW AND A FAST FORMULA 1 DRIVER. EVEN QUALIFYING TIMES SHOW ONLY MINUTE DIFFERENCES OF 10THS OR 100THS OF A SECOND. The key aspect is driving style:

The ability of a car to be steered derives from the adhesion of its tyres.... As soon as the car is being braked or driven, or as it changes direction, inertia forces are created which use up part of the available grip.

(Paul Frère, *Sports Car and Competition Driving*, 1963 (2nd ed. 1993), p. 35)

Grip is not only a result of tyres and their adhesion, but also the physical forces deriving from different car concepts driven through corners. In 1956, Clutton, Posthumus and Jenkinson described a rather striking example in *The Racing Car*:

The Ferrari 553 ... had a very chequered career mainly due to antipathy on the part of the drivers, for it had extreme understeer characteristics which demanded a new driving technique. The old Type 625 had been a very easy car to drive, and no one seemed keen to adapt themselves to the new technique.

A little later, however, drivers began to develop driving styles. In his autobiography, *Jim Clark at the Wheel*, the Scottish racing ace describes an unusual phenomenon:

Most people run deep into a corner before turning the wheels.... In this way you can complete all your braking in a straight line; ... but I prefer to cut into the

1960s Grand Prix racing saw drivers adopting their own cornering tecniques, Jim Clark (left) developed a 'turn-in' line, while Jackie Stewart (right) followed a clear-cut line.

corner early and, even with my brakes still on, to set up the car earlier.

Similarly, Frère states:

In order to reach the straight at a speed higher than the maximum speed compatible with a corner, we must adopt a line that is different....The new line follows a curve of variable radius. At the beginning, the new line will be more sharply curved than the original line... As soon as the curve starts to widen, the car can be accelerated as the progressive decrease of the curvature allows a progressive increase in its speed.

The idea behind all that, concluded Peter Windsor in his June 1997 column of *F1 Racing* magazine, is the 'Friction circle' as described by Mark Donohue in 1968:

A car ... has relatively equal traction capabilities in any direction, whether accelerating, braking or cornering. The theory is that you get maximum performance when you pass from one condition to the other without going through the 'centre of the circle'....The fastest way into a corner is gradually to trade off braking traction versus cornering traction.

Windsor differentiates between Jim Clark's 'turn-in' line (also applied by Alain Prost or Michael Schumacher) and classic drivers who follow a clear-cut line (Ayrton Senna, Jackie Stewart). A third group comprises oversteer drivers who literally dance in a racing car (Gilles Villeneuve, Keke Rosberg et al.).

Whether you love or hate this categorization – and many drivers are perhaps not even fully aware of it – the 1950s and 1960s clearly marked a more scientific approach to racing car driving.

Peter Gethin at Monza
Fastest ever and narrowest winning margin Grand Prix, 1971

HEN TRIPLE FORMULA 1 WORLD CHAMPION NIKI LAUDA, who now works as a consultant to Ferrari, was asked about the highlights and low points of his 1997 Formula 1 season, he said that the wet race at Spa was the best moment. His worst memories, however, are linked with the race at Monza. He describes the race, which saw David Coulthard overtake Jean Alesi in the pits and win the race in procession-like style as 'a joke. It was decided in the pits and showed Formula 1 at its worst.'

But Monza has seen much better times. Modern Grand Prix fans who are bored by such races would be absolutely delighted simply by a photo of the nail-biting 1971 finish in which winner Peter Gethin held a lead of only 1/100th of a second over Ronnie Peterson. A further 800th of a second back was François Cevert, followed by Mike Hailwood by another 900th of a second. All four drivers were within 0.18 of each other and crossed the finishing line almost simultaneously. Howden Ganley, in fifth place, was only 0.43 s further back. Thus, Gethin, whose short Grand Prix career shows few other extraordinary highlights, won at Monza by the narrowest winning margin in Grand Prix history.

The eye witnesses were so impressed by the dramatic race that they did not realize another important fact: on this day, 5 September 1971, Peter

Gethin won the fastest ever Grand Prix race with an average speed of 242.616 km/h (150.759 mph)

Both phenomena – the ultra-close battle and the enormous average speed – have to do with the unique architecture of this circuit, located north of Milan. The smooth shape of the 5.79 km (3.6 mile) track always hosted breathtaking high-speed battles with incredible average speeds. But fast circuits also mean slipstream battles which offer groups of drivers realistic chances to win. Already by 1967 and 1969, whole packs of cars crossed the finishing line extremely closely. Today, the cars' aerodynamics mean they are so sensitive that the turbulence prevents drivers from overtaking. Following closely, cars used to benefit from a tow. Now, this benefit is lost and overtaking becomes almost impossible because the turbulence reduces downforce whenever cars follow too closely.

But speed also means danger. In 1972, three chicanes were built, so the average lap times decreased dramatically – by 32 km/h (20 mph). Over the course of the years, the second Lesmo corner was tightened and the chicanes modified. Yet the development of Formula 1 cars progressed so quickly that Damon Hill managed a 239 km/h (148.59 mph) lap in 1993. Since the modification of the Curva Grande and the Lesmo corner in 1994, drivers apparently have not been able to break through the 236 km/h (147 mph) barrier. In 1999 the new technical rules will mean that the cars change dramatically. Narrower cars and grooved tyres will almost certainly slow them down by several seconds per lap. It seems as if the 242 km/h (150 mph) average of Peter Gethin will never be reached again.

Peter Gethin took the prize at the Monza Grand Prix in 1971 by the narrowest margin ever – 1/100th of a second.

Ronnie Peterson at Longbeach, exhibiting
the revolutionary 'ground-effect'
principle adopted by Lotus.

Lotus 79

Chapman's 'something for nothing' ground-effect car, 1978

CONSIDER I AM VERY FIT BUT THE G FORCES ARE difficult to bear, quite honestly. After five quick laps, I can't hold my head straight,' a driver admitted. Later on, a special structure which supports the helmet had to be bolted to the back of the cockpit. At the same event, another driver admitted to being on the verge of black-out a couple of times.

This is how vividly ground effect can be described. Jacky Ickx, quoted above, had serious trouble at his comeback in 1979. The Belgian Grand Prix star of the 1960s and 1970s replaced the injured Patrick Depailler at Ligier. For the first time, Ickx drove a car with a new principle that had been harnessed by Lotus: 'ground-effect'.

The knowledge that an optimization of the airflow improves lap times had already resulted in streamlined cars before the Second World War. Yet the idea of using airflow to create downforce found its way into Formula 1 fairly late: the first wings appeared only in 1968. A modern Grand Prix car creates far more than 1.5 tonnes of downforce – a multiple of the car's own weight, which means it could drive on a tunnel's ceiling.

But other solutions had to be found, because the rules soon limited the sizes of wings and, if you create downforce by angling the wings more and more, drag slows the car down. But Formula 1 would not be Formula 1 if its designers could not find loopholes. In 1962 the Lotus 25 was already a milestone in F1 engineering. Instead of the common tube frame chassis, it was based on a rigid, light and crash-resistant monocoque which allowed a far more sophisticated set-up of the suspension and superior cornering abilities. Formula 1 cars still have monocoques today, albeit of carbon fibre.

Fifteen years later, in 1977, Lotus founder Colin Chapman invented the 'wing car' principle in his Lotus 78, later to be upgraded in the 1978 Lotus 79 ground-effect car, in which the underfloor rises towards the rear end of the car. In addition, side-mounted 'skirts' form an airtight tunnel under the car. The channelled airflow creates a venturi effect which means there is a vacuum. Thus, the car is sucked to the track, which is the 'ground-effect'. Because of this superior adhesion, lap times did not improve gradually, but fell dramatically, by up to five seconds.

But Jacky Ickx's quote also reveals the dangers of the concept. Cornering speeds became far too high, and already, by 1981, 60 mm (2.36 in) ground clearance became mandatory and the skirts were banned, making the ground-effect negligible. In 1982 the skirts were reintroduced but were not allowed to touch the track: bizarre hydraulic suspensions circumvented this problem, producing serious stresses for the drivers' backs. Finally, in 1983 flat bottoms became mandatory. This seriously limited ground-effect in Formula 1, although the idea was continued in Group C sports cars.

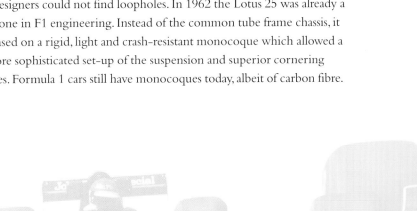

Triumph of the 'yellow teapot'
Jabouille's victory in the Renault RS10, 1979

DIJON, 1 JULY 1979, A COLD, OVERCAST AND DRY SUNDAY. WITH CLOCKWORK PRECISION, RENAULT DRIVER JEAN-PIERRE JABOUILLE REELS OFF THE FRENCH GRAND PRIX. The spectacle lasted 95 minutes, and about 100,000 spectators witnessed the historic triumph of the canary-yellow RS10-02. Was this a victory like all others? Yes and no. The gap of 15 seconds between Jabouille and Gilles Villeneuve's Ferrari came as no surprise.

More unusual, however, was the victory of a Frenchman in his home Grand Prix driving a French marque – the last time this happened was in 1927 when Robert Benoist won in his Delage.

But the Renault victory was exceptional because it marked a new era. 'After that victory, nobody ever dared to call the Renault the "yellow teapot" again,' quipped Jabouille. The whooshing, flame-spewing car was powered by a turbocharged engine – the first of its kind. Two little turbines the size of a saucepan were breathing new life into Grand Prix engines. This invention, already patented at the beginning of the century, uses the energy of the exhaust gases to generate power to compress fresh air into the combustion chambers. Additionally, more fuel is injected. Thus, the combustion is much more violent and the performance grows dramatically.

This solution, which had been allowable since 1966 but debuted in Grand Prix racing only in 1977, triggered a revolution – even if many remained doubtful. Quentin Spurring, then editor of the respected motor sports weekly *Autosport*, wrote:

'Inevitably, there were those in the paddock on Sunday evening who were forecasting "the end of Grand Prix racing as we know it" and so on.... We would not necessarily like to see a time when it became essential to have a turbo engine for competitiveness, nor do we think it will happen'.

A fallacy – because the potential of turbo engines turned out to be unpredictable. In its heyday, the power output was such that Renault was never able to measure it, as their test-benches would not have

Jean-Pierre Jabouille running away with the French Grand Prix in 1979 in his 'yellow teapot', with the first turbocharged engine.

put up with it. 'We estimate the figure to have been around 1200 bhp,' reckoned Technical Director Bernard Dudot.

BMW, Porsche, Ferrari and many others followed the new direction. In 1984, only five years after the first turbo victory, every Grand Prix was won by a turbo car. In 1986 normally aspirated engines were even banned. The performance of the turbo devils, however, was too hard to control despite tighter restrictions. By the end of 1988, their days were numbered. Normally aspirated engines celebrated a revival.

But the turbo era remains remarkable – Formula 1 engines never had this sheer brutality again. Today's machines are much smoother to drive – and much quicker. It is an irony that Renault never crowned its efforts with a World Championship title. After 20 victories, it ended its 10-year campaign in 1986. Only after its return in 1989 did the French turbo pioneer manage to clinch the title – six times in a row since 1992. With a non-turbo engine.

The Flying Finn's fastest ever qualifying lap

Keke Rosberg at the British Grand Prix, 1985

THE NAME KEKE ROSBERG HAS BECOME SYNONYMOUS WITH THE SPECTACULAR DRIVING STYLE EXERCISED BY HIS FINNISH RALLY COUNTRYMEN FOR MANY DECADES: flying with no mercy – without regard to road surface, grip or any other conditions physics wishes to dictate.

His victory in the 1983 Grand Prix of Monaco was one of the most remarkable examples of his art of driving. In that season, normally aspirated Cosworth engines gained the upper hand over the much more powerful turbo units only three times. One of these successes has to be credited to Keke, who drove like a daredevil through the damp streets of the principality, leaving his turbo-powered opponents a full 18 seconds behind. But the Finn who became World Champion in 1982 deserves a place in Grand Prix history for another reason: in 1985 he drove the fastest qualifying lap ever.

The contrast of the scenery could hardly have been greater: on the one hand, an old British wartime airfield at Silverstone, on the other, one of the most powerful Formula 1 cars ever built. Surprisingly, people already knew then that it would probably remain the fastest lap ever. 'Next time they come here the cars will perhaps be slower. Almost certainly the track will be changed,' noted Nigel Roebuck on 25 July in *Autosport* magazine. Indeed, in 1987, 1991 and 1994 further chicanes had been added to slow down the speeds – apparently the destiny of every modern GP circuit.

But the fairy-tale time in which the Finnish magician performed was the stuff of legends. It was the bizarre era of cars in extreme qualifying configurations. Qualifying trims still exist today but in 1986 the cars had several hundred horsepower more in qualifying than in racing specification.

Keke was beating the car around the 4.71 km (2.93 mile) circuit, braking lightyears too late for every corner and flying really hard over the kerbs of Woodcote. At 1:05.967 minutes came the break through the 257 km/h (160 mph) barrier. It had started to drizzle slightly and Keke ran wide in one chicane. 'No,' the Finn commented wryly. 'It was not because of the rain I ran wide. The car simply didn't turn in because I had a slow puncture on my left front wheel.' Ten minutes later, his mechanics were standing next to a tyre without any air....

The inevitable happened: the Finn went for a second attempt. Already Ayrton Senna, Nelson Piquet or Alain Prost were unable to match Rosberg's first time, but still he tried to improve on his own record. Would he succeed? Stowe corner was still damp, but Keke pushed as hard as he could, the Honda V6 unit producing a figure of more than 1000 horsepower.

This time, Keke achieved a time of 1:05.591 minutes – another 4/10ths quicker. This equals an average speed of exactly 258.928 km/h (160.925 mph). With this time, Keke Rosberg had beaten the opposition by 7/10 of a second. For ever.

Keke Rosberg making the fastest-ever qualifying lap in the 1985 British Grand Prix with an average speed of 258.928 km/h (160.925 mph).

The century's fastest racetrack
The argument rages on . . .

EN LOVE RECORDS. SINCE THE BEGINNING OF TIME THEY have tried to outdo each other in all kinds of competitions. They even write books about it. If you are looking for highlights in motor racing, you'll easily find them – the fastest races, the fastest laps, the most extreme qualifying times – but is there any chance of drawing a conclusion from this about the fastest track? If the fastest Grand Prix were a valid measurement, then Monza was the fastest track, because the 1971 race was won in a record 242.616 km/h (150.759 mph). Yet if your argument were based on the fastest ever

racing until 1960. The winner's speed was 223.276 km/h (138.767 mph) – no record, but a hint at the potential. Today, CART drivers do single laps of more than 386 km/h (240 mph). In the 1990 race, Arie Luyendyk achieved an average of 299.248 km/h (185.984 mph). Indy cars are, however, specially adapted to the oval circuits. A modern Grand Prix car would be slower.

Purists might say Indy never counted towards the Formula 1 World Championship standings, so let us ignore it as the quickest track. Another high-speed circuit was Avus. Tony Brooks won the 1959 race with an average speed of 230.619 km/h (143.331 mph). Though no absolute record, it was achieved fairly early by cars with rather small 2.5 litre engines. Again, the question arises: how quick would today's Formula 1 cars be on this track

Opposite: Michael Schumacher passes the chequered flag to win the 1996 Italian Grand Prix.

Left: the 1997 Italian Grand Prix at Monza, considered one of the fastest racetracks in the world.

qualifying lap, Silverstone would top your list: Keke Rosberg did a 258.928 km/h (160.925 mph) lap in 1985. Since then, though, tracks have changed. Tighter corners and additional chicanes slow down the cars.

If you reduce your perspective to the fastest circuit in use, the answer is simple: Monza. David Coulthard was quickest there in 1997 with 238 km/h (147.94 mph). But this is far too narrow an approach because it takes into consideration only the relatively quickest tracks each year. Moreover, the records are distorted by the permanent evolution of the cars and the regular cutbacks by new rules in order to slow them down.

So, was Monza in 1971 the fastest postwar Grand Prix track ever? Probably not, given that even the Indianapolis 500 was part of Grand Prix

at Berlin, given that its banked North Curve would still exist? Again, purists might argue that this track has never been a proper Grand Prix track for it hosted a GP only twice – in 1926 and 1959.

So we need to turn back to the fastest races in history. If you take the Top Ten races into account, Monza in 1970 and 1971 and in the early Nineties, as well as Spa-Francorchamps between 1968 and 1970, hosted the fastest races. If you extend your basis to the fastest laps, you have to add Silverstone in 1985 and 1987 to this list.

Hence the contest for fastest track ever, it seems, is between Italy, Belgium and Great Britain.

'The Professor'
Alain Prost's record 51 Grand Prix wins

HEN ALAIN PROST WAS RUBBING THE CHAMPAGNE OUT OF HIS EYES AFTER THE 1993 GRAND PRIX IN AUSTRALIA, HE KNEW THIS WAS THE LAST TIME. With his second place, he brought his career to a superb end after 13 seasons. The 'Professor', as the smooth Frenchman was nicknamed, had won a record 51 Grands Prix.

Back in 1980, he started his Formula 1 campaign with McLaren, scoring points in his first two Grands Prix. The British team was in a difficult period of transition, and after one season Prost joined Renault. Winning no fewer than nine times in the ensuing years, he soon became a formidable force. In 1983 he nearly won the title. Rejoining McLaren in 1984, Prost was beaten by Niki Lauda by only half a point. Yet the Frenchman was clearly quicker. In the following two seasons, Prost not only clinched two consecutive Championship crowns but outclassed his team-mates Lauda and Keke Rosberg. In 1987, however, the dominant Williams-Honda was invincible.

In the next season, McLaren secured the services of Honda and rising star Ayrton Senna. But the dream team soon turned into one of the fiercest duels in Formula 1, lasting until the end of Prost's career.

The Brazilian, who apparently had no interest in avoiding conflicts, soon turned McLaren into a hostile environment for Prost. Senna's World Championship win in his initial season with the team left no doubt about his skill, but his strong ego inevitably led to tension with Prost. The manner in which the Frenchman won his third championship in 1989 sparked off a long-lasting controversy. Senna tried to overtake in the last race, but Prost closed the door. They collided. Prost retired, whereas race winner Senna was disqualified afterwards – hence Prost became World Champion.

Feeling hounded by Senna, Prost swapped to Ferrari in 1990. Again, the title battle went right down to the wire, and in an almost carbon copy of 1989, a crash decided the outcome when the Brazilian deliberately collided with the Ferrari in order to win. The always outspoken Prost had become more and more political, using the media as a lever. Already at McLaren, he publicly accused Honda of heightening the tension artificially by supplying different engines to Senna. In 1991, the Scuderia Ferrari, suffering a difficult technical and political period, was on the receiving end. Prost's sharp criticism reached a peak on the penultimate round when he publicly called the car a 'lorry'. He was dismissed instantly and was forced to take a sabbatical in 1992.

In 1993, the clever Frenchman got the supreme Williams cockpit, his contract excluding Senna as team-mate. Prost won his fourth championship in undramatic style and retired after it was clear that Senna had a seat at Williams in 1994. Three years later, Prost founded his own outfit – Prost Grand Prix – when he acquired the Ligier team.

Perhaps a fifth title will be linked to the name of the quadruple World Champion some time in the future.

Right: Alain Prost celebrates winning the World Championship title – he competed in a total of 13 Grands Prix tournaments, with 51 wins.

Opposite: Prost driving his Ferrari in the 1991 US Grand Prix.

Ayrton Senna
Death of a superstar, May 1994

7 APRIL 1994, AIDA, JAPAN. THIRTY MINUTES BEFORE THE RACE, AYRTON SENNA WAS LYING MOTIONLESS ON THE FLOOR OF THE PADDOCK CABIN. He was just concentrating. Three years earlier, a reader of an F1 magazine observed Senna lying on the empty track at Hockenheim after practice, carefully studying a critical bump.

Ayrton Senna, a robot? Not quite. 'I had to keep my feelings very much under control because in those moments emotions were taking over ... making me feel very uneasy.'

That is what Senna said just before the start of his last race for McLaren.

He spent the most successful part of his career with the Woking outfit: 46 poles, 35 wins and three titles in six years. Six years in which the almost superhuman talent of the man with the strong religious beliefs was acknowledged by virtually everybody.

After having spent his first season with Toleman in 1984, showing a stunning performance at Monaco, and the following three with the quick but inconsistent Lotus team, he started his most successful period in 1988. McLaren won 15 out of 16 Grands Prix – Senna eight, Prost seven. Senna's main aim was to outdo his partner. 'Senna would have been quick in a wheelbarrow,' McLaren team manager Jo Ramirez reckons, 'whereas Prost had a better feeling for the set-up – initially.'

Psychologically, Senna had a problem with quicker team-mates. He outclassed his Lotus partners, but alongside quick drivers, he tended to overreact. At the 1988 Grand Prix of Portugal, the Brazilian felt he was blocked by his partner after the start, yet video analysis proved the opposite. After the restart, Prost overtook Senna who pushed him towards the pitwall.

In the 1989 Grand Prix of San Marino, Senna and Prost had an agreement: the one who leads in the first corner must not be attacked in the first lap. After a restart, Prost was quicker, but Senna overtook him. The Frenchman regarded it as a breach of their agreement, but Senna said they'd only been talking about the start, not the restart.

'Once at his home Grand Prix,' Ramirez recalled, 'Prost set a superb early qualifying time. He came in, changed and stood on the pitwall for the rest of the session. Ayrton, who couldn't find a suitable set-up, was totally demoralized. He was boiling. He could never accept anyone else was faster, whereas Alain could.' Senna's obsession and Prost's stubbornness came to a head in two risky incidents in the Grands Prix of Japan in 1989 and 1990, when they took each other off in order to become World Champion.

In 1993, Prost drove for top team Williams, his contract excluding Senna as team-mate. The Brazilian was furious, claiming that Prost couldn't stand a better partner. Prost became Champion, retired and Ayrton inherited the Williams cockpit. In his third Grand Prix for the team, Senna had his fatal accident at Imola on 1 May 1994.

Expert surveys regularly suggest that Senna was the greatest ever driver, but seasoned observers counter that his over-aggressive driving put him outside the class of Fangio, Moss or Clark.

Opposite: *one of the characters of the sport – Senna driving in the Belgium Grand Prix.*

Below: *Ayrton Senna (centre), celebrates with Alain Prost and Damon Hill – despite his successes, Senna had continual disagreements with his managers and team-mates.*

Scotland's Beatle-capped crusader
Jackie Stewart – safety-conscious Formula 1 ace

A SUNNY FRIDAY IN OCTOBER. AT A RESPECTABLE SPEED, TWO WHITE FORMULA 1 CARS ARE LAPPING SILVERSTONE NATIONAL CIRCUIT. TECHNICAL DIRECTOR ALAN JENKINS SMILES. 'There was a lot for him to get used to. He was still blipping the throttle on downchanges,' Jenkins says.

'He' was Jackie Stewart who had just sampled his own Formula 1 car together with his son, Paul. Blipping the throttle – that was something triple World Champion Jackie was brought up with. The white car he tested was a Stewart-Ford SF1, built 24 years after his last World Championship title in 1973.

Back in the 1950s, it did not quite look as if Jackie's sport would be motor racing. He was excellent at clay pigeon shooting, getting as far as the 1960 Rome Olympics. In the early 1960s, his motor racing career started at the wheel of GT and Touring cars and he soon entered Formula 3.

Right: Stewart keeps his hand in as manager of his own Grand Prix team.

Below: Jackie Stewart in his racing days.

He was offered his first chance in a Formula 1 car by Lotus founder Colin Chapman. After a one-off race, Stewart realised that Chapman had eyes only for his fellow Scot Jim Clark at Lotus, so he turned down an offer for 1965 and started with BRM. His first victory followed soon, at Monza, but after a poor time, he swapped to Matra in 1968. For the first time in a really competitive car, Jackie would have clinched the title had he not missed two races with a wrist injury. In that year, he showed a stunning performance at the Nürburgring, his winning margin in appalling conditions being 4 min 3 sec.

In 1969, he eventually scored his first title with six victories in a Matra MS80. With inferior machinery, he was not able to repeat his success in 1970. In the next year, Stewart easily won his second title with Tyrrell. An ulcer forced him to take six weeks out of the following season, letting the title slip to Emerson Fittipaldi.

1973 was Stewart's last season. Already by April, he had privately admitted his intention to retire. After his third title, he gave up his career at the early age of 34. Tragically, his team-mate François Cevert died in practice for what Jackie planned as his last GP – his 100th race, at Watkins Glen, but Tyrrell withdrew from the event.

The name of Jackie Stewart is linked not only with a brilliant career in which Jim Clark's record of 25 wins was topped by two, but also with a greater emphasis on safety in the sport. Stewart was the first to use seat belts and his BRM featured a spanner taped to the steering wheel to facilitate quick removal after he had been trapped in a fuel-leaking wreck at Spa in 1966. Ever since, he has remained famous for his outspoken safety campaigns. From 1997, he regularly attended each GP again – as the boss of his own Grand Prix team.

The most romantic name
Enzo Ferrari launches a legend

MORE THAN ANY OTHER TEAM, FERRARI HAS BEEN SHAPED BY ONE SINGLE PERSON, 'IL COMMENDATORE'. And more than any other team, Ferrari has left its mark on Grand Prix racing. Without Ferrari, Formula 1 seems impossible.

Enzo Ferrari, who used to race for Alfa Romeo, launched his own company in 1947. The myth that emerged within a few decades shines far brighter than any other team's.

A focal point was Ferrari's dedication. Tazio Nuvolari was an everlasting benchmark. This man from Mantova, whose career mainly took place before the Second World War, was a hero who could overcome almost all kinds of physical pain, driving with broken ribs or a broken leg on several occasions. The Commendatore judged all his Formula 1 drivers starting from this principle. Only one left a similar impression on him: Gilles Villeneuve. Ferrari called the Canadian 'the little prince', but his heroic career with the prancing horse lasted only 67 races – in 1982, the father of the reigning World Champion, Jacques, died at Zolder.

Much as that testifies to the warmth of Ferrari's character, his domineering nature was notorious. In his book *Das Dritte Leben* [The third life], double Ferrari World Champion Niki Lauda describes his negotiations with the old man:

'He was swearing at me and shouting himself hoarse, and afterwards he told the press: "Lauda is a Judas who sells himself to our opponents for thirty salamis."'

His patriarchical traits and the fact that he no longer attended races as he got older meant that the people surrounding him manipulated his impression of the GP scene. The successful Scuderia, which always faced highs and lows, clinched eight driver and eight manufacturer titles up to 1983. In the late 1980s and after Enzo's death in 1988, the team was in deep crisis. Even top drivers such as Nigel Mansell or Alain Prost could not lead the prancing horse to a World Championship – Jody Scheckter was the last Ferrari champion in 1979. Alain Prost fought for the title right down to the wire in 1990, but lost it. He fell out with the badly guided Scuderia in 1991, which dismissed him early.

With the arrival of Luca di Montezemolo, a slow process of restructuring began in 1992, although the influential Italian media and their intrigues continued to interfere. Di Montezemolo persuaded the successful ex-Peugeot rally manager Jean Todt to join the team, and in 1996 Michael Schumacher accepted a contract allegedly worth £25 million per year: all the ingredients for a successful package came together. It was a definitive turning point because the team already showed considerable progress in 1996. In the following season, the Ferrari proved a reliable machine for the German, who was a serious title contender until the end of the season, even if he failed to clinch the title in highly controversial circumstances.

It seems as if the Scuderia, whose budget is far superior to all the other teams', is finally recapturing the glory days of the past.

Since Enzo Ferrari launched his company in 1947, the Ferrari name has become renowned world-wide as one of the great Grand Prix teams.

Team Lotus
The triumph and the tragedy

WOULD IT BE FAIR TO DESCRIBE THE HISTORY OF LOTUS AS A STORY OF TRIUMPH AND TRAGEDY? Through gas turbines and wing cars, revolutionary monocoques and ground-effect, four-wheel drive and active suspension, the dual chassis and the pitiful end of the Lotus Formula 1 team, you can find 79 victories, but also many, many tragedies, including founder Colin Chapman's mysterious death in 1982.

In 1972, Emerson Fittipaldi won another World Championship crown. After a mediocre period in the mid-1970s, the next highlight followed with the types 78 and 79. The wing car and, later, the ground-effect car were other technical revolutions. This unconventional aerodynamic concept was rewarded with 13 wins in 1977–78. Mario Andretti clinched the title in 1978 – the last for the Norfolk-based team.

From then to 1984, Elio de Angelis scored only one single win for the team. After Chapman's death in 1982, Peter Warr took charge. The last successful phase from 1985 to 1987 saw seven victories, thanks both to turbo power from Renault and Honda and later to a revolutionary active suspension, which, combined with the skill of Ayrton Senna, was relatively successful.

After some barren years, the team was on the brink of mediocrity in 1990–91 when Peter Collins took over and led a buy-out. For a while, it looked as if the cars in the hands of Mika Häkkinen and Johnny Herbert were climbing back up the grid, but at the end of 1994 team went into administration and was closed down as a racing entity.

After 37 years and 491 Grands Prix, Lotus will always be remembered for its legendary milestones of engineering and the romance of the Clark era.

From its birth in 1952 to its closure in 1994, Lotus cars provided some of the most exhilarating, and dangerous, action in Grands Prix.

Anthony Bruce Colin Chapman founded his company on 1 January 1952. The first GP car, the front-engined Lotus 16 from 1958, was a rather conservative design and failed to win a single Grand Prix. Only the type 18, nicknamed 'biscuit box', helped make the breakthrough in 1960 when Stirling Moss took the first victory in a privateer car.

With Innes Ireland and particularly Jim Clark, a fabulous series of wins began, which was capped in 1963 and 1965 with two World Championship titles for Clark.

In 1968, Jim Clark had a fatal accident in a Formula 2 race, but Graham Hill won the World Championship title in the simple Lotus 49. This car, which debuted the Ford DFV engine in 1967, laid the basis for a second title in 1970. But when the wings of the Lotus 49 collapsed owing to the enormous downforce it generated, both Hill and Jochen Rindt crashed heavily.

Whereas the four-wheel drive Lotus 63 was a flop, the era with the Lotus 72 began in 1970, which was to bear the fruit of 20 victories and five titles until 1975. But the beginning of this period began tragically. Jochen Rindt died in the cockpit of the wedge-shaped car because something broke. Rindt still won the World Championship title, albeit posthumously.

McLaren International
A reputation for immaculate preparation

THINK OF THE MOST FAMOUS SPONSOR LIVERY IN GRAND PRIX RACING, AND YOU WILL AUTOMATICALLY THINK OF ONE PARTICULAR TEAM. The red-and-white chevron had adorned McLaren's Formula 1 cars since 1974. After 23 years, the colours are now silver, representing a different tobacco brand.

Briefly, in January 1997, at a 'sneak preview' before the current sponsor was presented, the McLaren-Mercedes MP4-12 was liveried in bright orange. This was a tribute to the origins of the team whose cars wore orange between 1968 and 1971. In 1958, founder Bruce McLaren came from New Zealand to Europe and, in 1959, he won his first Grand Prix as the youngest driver ever. In 1966, he formed his own Grand Prix team, for which he drove until his death testing his own CanAm sportscar in 1970.

Up to 1973 McLaren gained only eight wins, but the breakthrough came in the following year. The newly acquired Emerson Fittipaldi, World Champion 1972, became champion for the second time and helped McLaren to its first manufacturer's title. In 1975, the Brazilian was only runner-up in the M23, whereas 1976 was another McLaren year when James Hunt won the title.

From 1977 onwards, however, a regression was apparent. Sponsor Philip Morris eventually urged team principal Teddy Mayer to merge with Project Four Racing Ltd, the outfit of former mechanic Ron Dennis. His Formula 2 team gained its excellent reputation through immaculate preparation.

In November 1980, McLaren International was founded. Dennis employed John Barnard, who was developing a revolutionary carbon-fibre chassis. In the hands of John Watson, the MP4 soon showed a good

performance, and even though there was a freak moment when the team failed to qualify at Monaco in 1983, it was clearly moving back to its old form.

In 1984, Alain Prost and Niki Lauda made the team a dominant victor, winning 12 out of 16 races. One of the main reasons was TAG-Porsche power. Dennis had persuaded Mansour Ojjeh of the Saudi company TAG to finance the engine, which Porsche was to build.

In 1984, Lauda became World Champion, Prost making it three in a row for McLaren in 1985 and 1986. 1987 saw Williams driver Nelson Piquet winning the title, but Dennis was already prepared for the next step – Honda power and Ayrton Senna for 1988. It was a success which GP racing had hardly ever seen before – McLaren won 15 out of 16 races.

Senna became three-times World Champion at McLaren, but 1991 was the last successful year. After Honda pulled out at the end of 1992, the team relied upon Ford engines for one year. In spite of five victories in 1992 and 1993 respectively, Senna left the team. After 10 years, McLaren suddenly started the 1994 season without a World Champion behind the wheel. In 1995, it swapped to its fourth engine manufacturer in four years – Mercedes.

Only in 1997 has the long period of drought been ended – David Coulthard won two and Mika Häkkinen one Grand Prix. Slowly, the Woking giant is recovering again.

Left: Ayrton Senna in action for the McLaren team.

Below: David Coulthard qualifying for the Argentinian Grand Prix in the New McLaren GT.

Williams Grand Prix engineering
The sweet smell of success

HEN WILLIAMS CELEBRATED ITS CENTURY OF FORMULA 1 victories at the British Grand Prix in 1997, a historical landmark had been reached. The teams with a three-digit figure of GPs constitute a small, élite club. Only McLaren and Ferrari have more victories – 106 and 113 respectively by the end of 1997.

Thirty years back, the team did not start quite so successfully. In 1969, Frank Williams entered a Formula 1 car for the first time – a Brabham for his friend Piers Courage. After Courage's death in 1970, the Englishman prepared a March for Henri Pescarolo. His budget was very weak, though. 'I remember when Frank Williams had to borrow money each month to pay the wages,' recalls senior French journalist Jabby Crombac. 'Once, when Williams couldn't find it, he offered his clothes to his mechanics.' Before going completely bankrupt, Williams's enterprise was saved by Canadian oil magnate Walter Wolf. Thus the cars became Wolf cars – something Frank was not exactly enthused about.

In 1977, Williams was his own boss again, entering a March 771. Sponsorship contracts with the Saudi-Arabian airline Saudia, the Albilad trading company and the high-technology Franco-Saudi company Techniques d'Avant Garde (TAG) helped Williams to build his own cars from 1978, starting with the FW 06. Williams hired a young engineer and made him shareholder: Patrick Head.

At the Grand Prix of Europe in October 1997, Williams and Head were still conducting the Williams orchestra and ended the season with a double World Championship title.

What happened in the two decades between the FW06 and the FW19 is an unprecedented success story. With Alan Jones, Keke Rosberg, Nelson Piquet, Nigel Mansell, Alain Prost, Damon Hill and Jacques Villeneuve, Williams had seven World Champions and won nine manufacturer's titles – more than Ferrari who had only won eight titles since the introduction of the Championship in 1958.

One of the characteristic traits of founder Frank Williams is his strength of mind. In 1986, he sustained spinal injuries in a car crash which left him paralysed. Yet his team managed to clinch the manufacturer's title in that year and, as early as 1987, Williams started taking up his position again although it had temporarily looked as if he had no chance of survival.

After a tough season in 1988, Williams teamed up with Renault in 1989: it was the beginning of the most successful era for the engine manufacturer and the team. From 1992, they gained five Constructors' Championships. Patrick Head's design department became an élite school for engineers who are very much sought after, such as Adrian Newey who recently swapped to McLaren.

After a period of overwhelming success, Renault pulled out of Formula 1 at the end of 1997, handing over its business to subsidiary Mecachrome and leaving Williams with a somewhat unclear future. From 2000 onwards, however, BMW will supply engines so that Williams can fulfil its dream of remaining the team with the highest ratio of wins per entry.

Top: *Frank Williams and Patrick Head watch the times during practice.*

Bottom: *Nigel Mansell in his Williams Renault – a successful collaboration.*

Opposite: *the Williams race: Jacques Villeneuve leads Damon Hill in practice for the Brazilian Grand Prix.*

Grand Prix Greats

The 10 fastest laps in Grand Prix history (since 1950)

Key: *Driver, manufacturer, car, venue, date, speed and lap.*

1. DAMON HILL (Williams-Renault FW15C), *Monza, 12 September 1993, 249.782 km/h (155.241 mph) on lap 45.*

At Monza, Hill celebrated his third win in his first season with Williams. His fastest lap is very hard to match because the track has been changed since.

2. HENRI PESCAROLO (March 711 Cosworth), *Monza, 5 September 1971, 246.963 km/h (153.489 mph) on lap 9.*

Frenchman Pescarolo managed his fastest lap in a year when the arrival of slick tyres and airboxes made the cars much quicker, even though many doubted the accuracy of the lap timing for the French journeyman. Since 1972, chicanes have slowed down the speeds at Monza.

3. NIGEL MANSELL (Williams–Honda FW11B), *Silverstone 12 July 1987, 246.271 km/h (153.059 mph) on lap 58.*

Combine the speed of one of the most powerful cars in F1 history with the skill of Nigel Mansell and the Silverstone track before the introduction of major revisions in 1991, and you'll get this fantastic lap.

4. MIKA HÄKKINEN (McLaren–Mercedes MP4-12), *Monza, 7 September 1997, 244.886 km/h (152.198 mph) on lap 49.*

Is the ultrafast Finn Mika Häkkinen beginning to catch up with the two names topping this list? It seems modern GP cars have started to overcome the detrimental effects of chicanes on lap times at Monza.

5. CHRIS AMON (March 701 Cosworth), *Spa-Francorchamps, 7 June 1970, 244.691 km/h (152.077) mph on lap 28.*

Amon achieved his 152 mph lap during the last Grand Prix on the old, superfast 14.096 km (8.761 mile) track. In 1979, a new 6.9 km (4.3 mile) circuit was built which hosted the Belgian Grand Prix in 1983 and since 1985.

6. ALAIN PROST (McLaren MP4/2B), *Silverstone, 21 July 1985, 243.015 km/h (151.035 mph) on lap 43.*

In the year when he won his first out of four World Championship titles, Alain Prost drove the fastest lap at Silverstone and won the British Grand Prix, which was stopped early in error.

7. DAMON HILL (Williams FW16B), *Monza, 11 September 1994, 242.936 km/h (150.986 mph) on lap 24.*

In a year when he lost his team–mate Ayrton Senna in a fatal accident, Hill set the fastest lap time at Monza, won there and fought for the Championship right until the end – but lost it.

8. CLAY REGAZZONI (Ferrari 312B), *Monza, 16 August 1970, 242.905 (150.967 mph) on lap 65.*

In the penultimate year before the introduction of chicanes at the circuit, Ferrari driver Regazzoni set not only the quickest lap but scored his maiden victory at Monza in his first Grand Prix season.

10. AYRTON SENNA (McLaren-Honda MP4/6), *Monza, 8 September 1991, 241.446 km/h (150.060 mph) on lap 41.*

The legendary Brazilian won his last championship in 1991, and many think it was the hardest fought and most deserved title because the new V12 Honda engine was not very highly respected.

9. JEAN-PIERRE BELTOISE (Matra MS80 Cosworth), *Monza, 7 September 1969, 242.905 km/h (150.967 mph) on lap 64.*

The first four in the 1969 Italian Grand Prix finished within less than 2/10ths of a second of each other. The fastest lap has been credited to third-placed Jean-Pierre Beltoise.

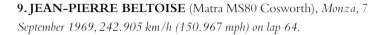

Indy Car Racing

4

You don't let anything get in your mind to get in the way, you just concentrate and go, go, go.

Rex Mays, Indy 500 winner

Birth of the Brickyard
American motor sport is born, May 1911

THE CURRENT DETROIT-BASED STATESIDE MOTOR INDUSTRY HAS ITS ROOTS IN THE BACKWATER OF INDIANAPOLIS, NICKNAMED 'INDIA-NO-PLACE'. By 1910, the city was home to over 60 car manufacturers, so it seemed logical that a motor race should be staged here.

The man who set the ball rolling was a local entrepreneur called Carl Fisher. He saw in 1908 how it would benefit the assembled manufacturers to have a local test track to raise the image of their products by staging races. He had seen the Gordon Bennett Trophy races in Europe and was thrilled by the speed and spectacle.

Overleaf: the Penske team holding the front row of the grid in 1988 (see page 95).

Right: the development of the Indy racing car from the first Indianapolis 500 in 1911 – when only 10 of the 44 entries finished the race – to the modern day.

The result was a 4.023 km (2.5 mile) oval completed in two months, whose track surface consisted of about three and a half million bricks cemented together; hence it was known as 'the Brickyard'.

Such a circuit needed a showcase event, and Fisher was characteristically pragmatic. Spectators wanted a spectacle that would push men and machinery to the limit, yet even the most hardened race fans get tired. It was decided that about six hours' racing would fall within the average person's enjoyment threshold, which at the speeds of the day equated to approximately 500 miles. The stage was set for the first

Indianapolis 500 on 11 May 1911.

Forty-four entries arrived for the first qualifying session on 1 May. The rules were simple: those who could average 120 km/h (75 mph) or more through the speed traps were in.

Perhaps the most controversial entry was that of car number 32, a Marmon Wasp piloted by Ray Harroun. It differed radically from the rest in that it did not carry a second seat for a mechanic and the driver himself sat in the middle rather than the back of the car. Furthermore, the Marmon was very narrow and it had a distinctive tapering tail which narrowed to a sharp point at the rear. The overall effect was that of a man driving a very fast and noisy cigar. It was approximately 10 per cent more powerful than the other 'Indy cars', benefiting from a six-cylinder 7817 cc engine producing 110 hp, enabling this leviathan to crack 160 km/h (100 mph) on the straight – blindingly fast when you consider that the turn of the century was a comparatively recent memory.

Unfortunately, other drivers protested Harroun's car on the grounds that there was no passenger to watch for oncoming traffic; a problem easily solved when Harroun attached a rear-view mirror. A trivial incident, but that was the first racing modification made in history to enable a car to compete at Indianapolis.

Harroun won comfortably in 6 hr 42 min 8 sec, despite the fact that other cars had larger engine displacements. Ralph Mulford, in a Lozier, took the runner-up spot, over a minute behind Harroun, and after that there was an enormous gap of nine minutes to the third-placed Hewlett-Fiat of David Bruce-Brown. There were only 10 finishers – a testament to the gruelling nature of this endurance classic.

'The only true sport'
Indy gets faster … and faster, 1925

THE WINNER OF THE ORIGINAL INDIANAPOLIS 500 IN 1911, RAY HARROUN, MANAGED TO AVERAGE A SPEED OF 120.04 KM/H (74.602 MPH) DURING THE RACE. HIGHLY IMPRESSIVE, but in all forms of motor sport continuing technology inevitably dictates

that average speeds will rise. Indeed, in Formula 1 the FIA (Fédération Internationale de l'Automobile, Formula 1's governing body) has continually tried to reduce speeds by banning ground-effect, turbos, traction control, ABS and by reducing engine size … and still cars have been going quicker and quicker each year!

The increase in average speeds at the Indianapolis 500 makes interesting reading: in 1912 Joe Dawson's National won at a speed of 126.68 km/h (78.72 mph), but the following year, the average speed of the winner, Jules Groux, dropped to 122.202 km/h (75.933 mph). In 1914, Rene Thomas's Delage cracked the 128 km/h (80 mph) barrier comfortably, and in 1915, Ralph de Palma's Mercedes came within a whisker of cracking 144 km/h (90 mph), averaging 144.58 km/h (89.84 mph) over the race.

Many people came close, but the 144 km/h (90 mph) barrier was not finally beaten until 1922, when Jimmy Murphy triumphed, having driven his evocatively named Duesenberg-Miller at an average of 152.05 km/h (94.48 mph), an increase of 8 km/h (5 mph) over the previous year's winning time.

Perhaps the following year would prove the milestone event to beat the magic 160 km/h (100 mph)? But it was not to be. Instead fanatics had to wait until the 1925 event.

Peter de Paolo won magnificently, driving a 122 cubic inch Duesenberg. His victory was made all the sweeter on learning that he had managed to average a speed of 162.75 km/h (101.13 mph) over the 4 hr 56 min 39 sec he had been driving. To have kept going for that long in a noisy, vibrating car where every fibre of your being is exposed to the elements is worthy of a prize in itself.

Seat belts on the Indy cars of that era were optional, as contemporary thinking was that in the event of an accident it was best to be thrown clear of the car. In any case, there would be no safety fences, fire extinguishers or roll bars to save any luckless driver who happened to crash his car. A hundred miles per hour may not sound fast in modern racing terms, but it was incredibly fast and incredibly dangerous back then.

Second-placed man at the 1925 race, Dave Lewis, driving a Junior 8-R, also managed to average more than 160 km/h (100 mph). Phil Shafer, who came third, was another to crack that magic barrier, in another Duesenberg.

De Paolo's feat was such that an average Indianapolis winning speed greater than the ton was not seen again until 1930, when Billy Arnold's Miller-Hartz special did 161.655 km/h (100.448 mph).

Ernest Hemingway once said that race-car driving and bull-fighting were the only two true sports. On that day in 1925, the heroic Peter de Paolo in car number 12 perhaps proved that to be true.

Above: the winner of the first race in 1911, Ray Harroun.

Left: Peter De Paolo with his Duesenberg in which he won the 1925 Indy 500.

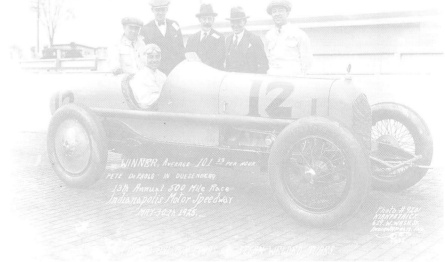

'Super-sub'

Frank Lockhart's one-lap qualifying record, May 1926

A ONE-LAP QUALIFYING RECORD OF 115.488 MPH WAS SET ON THE 20 MAY 1926 BY THE INTREPID FRANK LOCKHART.

Qualifying records are set on almost a yearly basis at the Indianapolis 500, so one could be forgiven for thinking that, although very impressive, there was nothing particularly special about Frank Lockhart's achievement. There is more to it than meets the eye, though, as Frank Lockhart was never intended to drive the Miller that set the record. The intended driver was Peter Kreis, who found himself too unwell to drive at very short notice, so his friend Lockhart grasped the nettle, despite never having previously driven at Indianapolis before.

Lockhart had some racing experience but he had never driven a Miller and was able to seize only a few days' practice before being called upon to set a qualifying time. He amazed onlookers with his astonishing one-lap record in car number 15. Having started from 20th on the grid and made an excellent start, he climbed rapidly up the order, and he engaged the previous year's winner, Peter de Paolo, in an excellent duel which lasted over 20 laps. In a perfect end to the fairy tale, Lockhart went on to win the race by over 40 seconds from the second-placed car of Harry Hartz, who was also driving a Miller Special. In total, Lockhart drove for 4 hr 10 min 14 sec, during which he maintained an average speed of 153.343 km/h (95.904

In 1926, Frank Lockhart, who had never driven the Miller before, set the one-lap qualifying record, then went on to win the race.

mph) in the rain-shortened race. Cliff Woodbury, driving a Boyle, finished third – a minute and a half behind Lockhart. As for the famous Peter de Paolo, he finished fifth, after his engine lost performance towards the end of the race.

Having shown that he clearly possessed an aptitude for driving at Indianapolis, Frank Lockhart set another one-lap qualifying record in 1927. This time he was driving a Perfect Circle Miller, with which he managed to set a lap speed of 194.598 km/h (120.918 mph). In the same year he also set a four-lap record speed of 193.282 km/h (120.100 mph). He was less fortunate in the race, however, retiring after 120 laps with an overheating engine. George Souders's Duesenberg was the winner – but only just – from Earl de Vore's Miller.

The irony is that Peter Kreis, for whom Lockhart raced, never achieved further distinction in Indy cars, retiring from the races that he contested in 1927 and 1928. Lockhart had a comparatively brief career, but he is remembered more for what he did achieve than for what he did not.

The 1997 Formula 1 season was known as the 'year of the super sub' owing to the highly impressive performances of Alex Wurz and Jarno Trulli who substituted for Gerhard Berger and Olivier Panis respectively. Lockhart is proof that the concept of the 'super sub' is not necessarily a modern one.

'Just concentrate and go, go, go'
Four-lap qualifying record, May 1990

THE QUALIFYING PROCEDURE FOR THE INDIANAPOLIS 500 IS VERY DIFFERENT FROM THAT USED IN MOST MOTOR RACES. There are 33 grid positions up for grabs, which are determined by qualification sessions that take place on the two weekends immediately preceding the race.

A qualification run consists of four consecutive timed laps at speed (following two warm-up laps). The unique aspect is that the drivers are dispatched from the waiting line one at a time, with no other cars on the track while they attempt to set their time. This ensures a totally fair competition, as it is just the driver, his car and the track and permits no Formula 1-style excuses of 'I could have set pole but I was blocked on my best lap'!

Equally, this system leads to more pressure, particularly when all the eyes of the Speedway are focused on the lone driver trying his utmost to break on to that magical front row.

'To get a good qualifying lap, you have to focus on just one thing: you get that car round that track just as quick as you can, you don't let anything get in your mind to get in the way, you just concentrate and go, go, go – but you make sure you don't make no mistakes neither.' These were the words of the legendary Rex Mays, who had been a five-time front-row starter by the time he was 28.

Arie Luyendyk had always been fast, as his victory in the 1990 Indianapolis 500 proved, but he proved just how resilient he was on 12 May 1996. The hot favourites for pole position and the race were the Menard team of Scott Brayton, Tony Stewart and Eddie Cheever.

Luyendyk astounded onlookers with a qualifying speed of 375.604 km/h (233.390 mph), putting him comfortably ahead of the opposition, and causing great consternation to rival team owner John Menard.

On Pole Day, however, Luyendyk's luck changed for the worse. He was nearly eliminated in a practice accident with Johnny Parsons and then learnt that his previous times were going to be excluded on the grounds that he was running an underweight car.

Undeterred at having missed his chance to qualify in the top 20, he bounced back on Sunday, 12 May, to set a track speed record over four laps of 385.051 km/h (239.260 mph). Remarkably, this also included a one-lap qualifying record of 382.215 km/h (237.498 mph).

'Today just makes up for the disappointment of yesterday,' said Luyendyk. 'It bugs me that we have to start so far back, in 21st, but we knew the rules going in. It's going to be difficult. I'll just be careful and pick my way through traffic.'

In the end, Luyendyk was not quite careful enough, retiring after an accident on lap 149. Victory went to Buddy Lazier, but with his four remarkable laps, Luyendyk had laid claim to his share of the glory.

Arie Luyendyk celebrating his four-lap qualifying record in 1990. Despite this, he was unable to take the title.

'...*like riding a bullet fired from a gun*'

Luyendyk's 220 mph Indy Racing League lap, 1997

THE GREAT ARIE LUYENDYK COULD NOT HAVE ASKED FOR ANYTHING MORE AT THE 1997 INDIANAPOLIS 500. RARELY HAS A MAN MADE HIS MARK ON THE EVENT SO CONVINCINGLY.

The more astute pundits had predicted that Luyendyk would be a formidable force, but he confounded their wildest expectations. His lap at 354.533 km/h (220.297 mph) on 5 May was the sort of lap that sends shivers down the pit lane. 'How can he go so fast?' was the question on everybody's lips, but he just smiled enigmatically.

He certainly had a good car: the highly rated British G-Force chassis mated with the Aurora 4 litre V8 engine was considered to be the best all-round combination. He was racing for the Treadway team, whose attention to detail is legendary.

New regulations for 1997 meant that the cars were not as quick as the previous years' examples, but that did not make them any less difficult to drive. 'It's like riding a bullet fired from a gun,' explained Indy car rookie Vincenzo Sospiri of the Indianapolis circuit. 'Then, when you get into the corners, you're trying to get back into the barrel.' Sospiri was highly impressive on his debut, securing third on the grid.

Luyendyk's four-lap run of 351.260 km/h (218.263 mph) was enough for him to secure the pole position he was denied the previous year because of a technical infringement. 'It's different now, more nervous,' said Luyendyk of the 1997 specification Indy Racing League car. 'The old cars had more grip and gave you more confidence. But you just have to get on and do the job.'

His comments were borne out by crashes in practice to Scott Sharp and John Paul Junior, both of whom hit walls after spinning. In each case, the crashes were attributed to the fact that not enough heat had been worked into the cars' tyres.

The race itself was somewhat fraught, having been rained off on the Sunday and again on the Monday. During the 15 laps that were completed on Monday, Luyendyk managed to lose his lead to Tony Stewart, when he became embroiled with a backmarker.

Tuesday saw the race restarted, and Luyendyk ran steadily behind Stewart before retaking the lead on lap 83 – only to have it taken from him again! Following a period of yellow flags, Luyendyk then found his team-mate, Canadian Scott Goodyear, in front of him. In a worryingly fearless manoeuvre, Luyendyk overtook Goodyear on the outside of turn three. Thereafter, the two Treadway drivers duelled all the way to the chequered

flag, but it was Luyendyk who got there first by 0.570 seconds, after 3 hr 25 min 43 sec.

Luyendyk was overjoyed to claim his second Indianapolis win: 'It was great, but hard work!,' he grinned. 'I had to run fast all day to stay in the lead compared to 1990. My last win came seven years ago under CART regulations. This race shows that the Indy Racing League formula does work.'

Seven years after his incredible four-lap qualifying record, Arie Luyendyk took the Indy 500 title after a nail-biting race.

A. J. Foyt
Foyt – spelt 'F OYT', pronounced 'Indy'

ANTHONY JOSEPH FOYT, JR, IS THAT RARE CREATURE, A genuine living legend. No man has quite dominated the Indy car scene the way he has and it seems likely that no other ever will.

Consider the raw statistics: he is the first man to have won the Indy 500 four times and the only driver to have achieved a hat-trick of wins at the Indy 500, Daytona 500 and Le Mans 24 Hours. He qualified for a record 35 consecutive Indy 500s and won 67 Indy Car races, with seven National Championships. No other racing driver – not even the great Fangio, with his five World Championships and 24 wins – can come anywhere close to this breathtaking achievement.

The remarkable thing is that Foyt did not stop there. He also has seven NASCAR Winston Cup victories, 41 USAC stock car wins, and a further 50 sprint car, midget and dirt champ wins. From the Indianapolis starts alone he is estimated to have earned $2,637,963.

He was born in Texas on 16 January 1935, and his glittering career came to an end in May 1993 at Indianapolis, the circuit he made his own. As he said himself: 'You don't know me from winning Daytona three times. You don't know me winning Le Mans. You don't know me winning Ontario. You don't know me winning Pocono four times. You know me from one place. And that's right here.'

Of course a man with such a dedication to the sport could not stay retired in his Texas cattle ranch for long. He entered racing again, this time as a team owner. A. J. Foyt Racing used a Dallara-Aurora in 1997, and the team for the Indianapolis 500 featured highly rated rookie Billy Boat.

The first time 'AJ' won the event himself was in 1961, driving the Bowes Seal Fast Special. The laurels went his way again in 1964, with the Sheraton Thompson Special, at an average speed of 237.136 km/h (147.350 mph). He completed a hat-trick with his 1967 victory, this time in his own Coyote Ford, thereby equalling Mauri Rose's record 'triple' (who won in 1941, 1947 and 1948).

Remarkably, A. J. Foyt took a fourth Indianapolis 500 victory 10 years after his previous win, carting off the purse after having driven magnificently, his Coyote-Ford averaging 259.537 km/h (161.331 mph) – 16 km/h (10 mph) faster than his 1967 win.

In 1975, Foyt tied with Rex Mays as a four-time pole winner, and he amazed everybody in 1991 by being a whisker away from taking pole again – and this after a huge accident the previous season that had smashed his legs! Foyt had also taken the qualifying runner-up spot in 1963 and 1978. This means that he had an incredible eight starts from the front row and a further eight starts from the second row!

He holds the record for the greatest number of racing miles pounded across the Indianapolis bricks: 12,272.5 miles (19,750 km) – that's about half the circumference of the earth.

Having led more '500s' than any other (13), the legendary 'AJ' can justifiably look back and reflect, in that soft Texan accent of his: 'ain't bad t'all'.

The legendary A. J. Foyt has won the Indianapolis 500 four times, and has ensured his name is amongst the Indy greats forever.

Arie Luyendyk
The fastest man on tyres in Indianapolis

THE GREAT ARIE LUYENDYK IS OFFICIALLY THE QUICKEST MAN EVER TO HAVE SET TYRES ON INDIANAPOLIS: a truly monumental achievement when you consider just how many illustrious racers have been there.

His detractors will immediately say that this is down to his machinery, but the last few years of racing have shown that competition now is closer than ever, so the emphasis has consequently fallen back upon the driver.

Arie Luyendyk has developed very consistently as a driver; every time you think he has reached his plateau, he pulls something still more astonishing out of the bag.

But his finest day to date has been 9 May 1996. That was the day when, in Jonathan Byrd's Reynard-Ford, Luyendyk achieved a track speed of 385.051 km/h (239.260 mph) during practice. The simple truth is that nobody has been quicker since. He was helped by optimal track conditions and a car that was obviously performing well, particularly, he mentioned, coming out of corners. As the Indianapolis circuit basically consists of left-hand corners, it is vital to have a good set-up, which includes ensuring that the right-hand side of the car (which bears the brunt of the cornering load) is properly stiffened in terms of suspension and tyre pressures.

'Actually, it felt quick but not mind-blowing. I was trying to go quickly, sure, but I didn't expect this,' said a relaxed Luyendyk immediately afterwards. But those were the words of a man who rightly feels he has little left to prove.

Born in Scottsdale, Arizona, on 21 September 1953, he now has two Indianapolis 500 victories under his belt, which have earned him in excess of $3 million. He is widely acknowledged as one of the fastest and most versatile racers around, which is why team owner Chip Ganassi had no hesitation in asking Luyendyk to replace bruised 1997 CART Champion Alex Zanardi at the final race of the 1997 season.

Luyendyk was highly impressive, having been forced to start from the back of the grid because he did not have an opportunity to qualify the car. He was making his inexorable way up the field, before rookie Arnd Meier spun in front of him, causing an inevitable collision.

Luyendyk is now considered an elder statesman, and he has done a lot of work to ensure that continuing safety developments are carried out within the Indy Racing League. In September 1997 he said: 'I signed again for Treadway Racing next year, but if they don't change the cars to make them safer, I can always change my mind. I don't mind hitting the wall, but there is a reason to be concerned. It seems that every time somebody hits the wall they go to hospital.'

The fact that the cars have been modified for the 1998 season is due in no small way to Luyendyk's outspoken comments. It was confirmed in October 1997 that Luyendyk would drive in the 1998 Indy Racing League.

Arie Luyendyk in his Indy car – he is now acknowledged as one of the greatest Indy drivers in the history of the race.

Il Leone roars
Nigel Mansell and his Lola-Chevrolet T9300

NIGEL MANSELL BURST ON TO THE INDY CAR SCENE ON 21 MARCH 1993, BECOMING THE FIRST EVER INDY CAR ROOKIE TO TAKE POLE POSITION AND VICTORY ON HIS RACE DEBUT. The only other driver to have won his first Indy race was Graham Hill in 1966 (though there are many who believe that Jim Clark really won that race as well as the 1965 event).

Having accomplished his ambition to win the Formula 1 World Championship, which he had been threatening to do since 1986, his well-publicized split with the Williams team led to the new challenge of Indy car racing. For Mansell it was a whole new departure: a change of job, with a different series of skills to learn and a change of address as he moved himself, wife Rosanne and their children to a new home in Clearwater, Florida.

Mansell's Formula 1 record has been characterized by spectacularly skilful driving and his reputation speaks for itself. Having fought his way up through Formulas Ford and Three he was spotted by the late Colin Chapman, head of Lotus, and made his Grand Prix debut in 1980.

In 1985 Mansell signed for the Williams team and won two consecutive victories at Brands Hatch and Kyalami. He won more races than any other driver in 1986, but lost the title to Prost by a mere two points after a spectacular tyre failure in the final race. In 1987, Mansell won six races to team-mate Piquet's three, but the Brazilian took the title by a narrow margin. In 1991 Mansell was runner-up to Senna, but in 1992 he finally clinched that elusive championship with five of the season's 16 races still to come. His nine wins in the season constituted a record, which was equalled by Michael Schumacher in 1995.

In Italy, when he was driving for the fabled Ferrari team, he was known as 'Il Leone' ('the Lion') for his fearless ability to scythe through traffic. But this wealth of experience did not prevent what was literally a baptism of fire when he crashed heavily in testing at the Phoenix. The force of the impact was such that the gearbox punched a hole through the solid concrete retaining wall.

Mansell's mount for the 1993 season was the Newman Haas team's Lola-Chevrolet T9300. In line with the regulations, the engine it used was a 2647 cc turbocharged V8, running on methanol, which produced about 850 bhp at 12,800 rpm. What the abstract figures fail to convey is the fact that the car had the potential to accelerate to 96 km/h (60 mph) in 2 sec, then on to 160 km/h (100 mph) in a further 2 sec. Top speed? Some 386 km/h (240 mph). That'll do nicely, sir.

It certainly did nicely for Nigel. He scored five wins over the 1993 season, four of them on the unknown quantity of oval tracks. He clinched the title with a win on the penultimate round, at Nazareth, Pennsylvania, to the delight of his many fans all over the world. 'I'm just thrilled to bits to win this one,' commented an ecstatic Mansell. 'It's very special.'

Nigel Mansell crashes against the wall during practice at the Phoenix Oval – this did not stop the man nicknamed 'Il Leone' in testimony to his fearlessness.

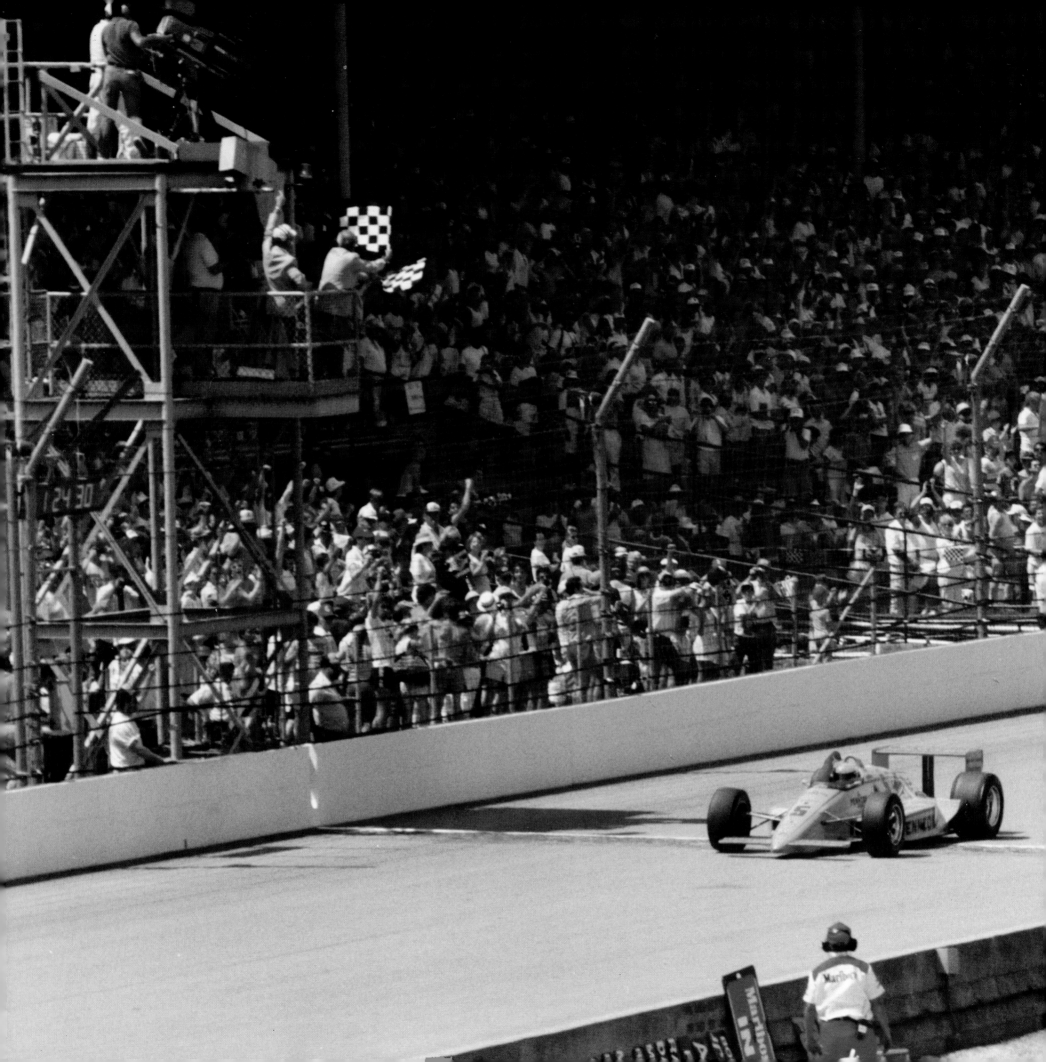

'Thrill of a lifetime'
Rick Mears – four-time Indy 500 winner

ICK MEARS IS ONE OF THE SELECT FEW TO HAVE EQUALLED A.J. FOYT'S RECORD OF FOUR INDIANAPOLIS 500 WINS, A TASK WHICH IS ABOUT AS EASY AS CONVERTING THE POPE TO BUDDHISM. He is also the person to have made most money out of the Indianapolis 500, scooping up $4,299,392 in prizes from his total of 14 starts. But it is not the loot that motivates the man behind the crash-helmet. In 1993 he wrote:

'There is nothing more thrilling in a driver's career than winning the Indianapolis 500. I hope that all the drivers and teams will be able to experience that thrill of a lifetime – to all of you, thanks for the memories'.

He won his last Indy 500 in 1991, overtaking leader Michael Andretti on the outside of a bend at 370 km/h (230 mph). 'Rick's going into the wall!,' screamed the commentator, but instead Rick went into the record books to claim his fourth Indianapolis win. 'The fourth win, it capped all the others,' he reminisced later. 'It was special for a lot of reasons.'

Mears is still closely associated with the Penske team headed by the outspoken Roger Penske, a worthy recipient of the nickname 'Mr Indianapolis'. About 15 years ago Penske stated, 'I'm not interested in second place, my cars have to win,' something that the extraordinary talent of Mears made possible four times at Indianapolis. In 1988, the Penske team made history by monopolizing the front row of the grid with Mears on pole, followed by Danny Sullivan and Al Unser. A familiar scenario, as Mears was the greatest qualifier in Indy history: the only driver to have taken pole position six times (in 1979, 1982, 1986, 1988, 1989 and 1991). In fact, he occupied a front-row starting position a record 11 times. Mears qualified on the front row

for his debut Indy 500 in 1978, where he was named 'Rookie of the Year'. His first pole position came the following year, at the expense of Tom Sneva.

Yes, but how about championships? Mears won three, in 1979, 1981 and 1982. For the record, he was victor of 29 Indy car races, which made him the most successful driver of the 1980s with 20 wins during the decade. Nearly 30 years on, Mears still seems slightly surprised by it all: 'I never dreamed of going to Indy. It just wasn't one of my goals.'

Mears was originally an off-road racer and was entered for the 1977 Indianapolis 500 with an uncompetitive car that failed to qualify. Plucked from relative obscurity by Roger Penske in 1978, he never looked back.

In December 1992, at a Penske Christmas party in Philadelphia, Mears announced his intention to retire from racing, having had a frustrating season punctuated by a nasty crash in Indy practice.

'Walking into a race will be a tug,' said Mears of his newly retired status, 'but I feel fortunate that we had that many opportunities. We got the most out of what we did.'

Opposite: *Rick Mears takes the chequered flag at the Indianapolis speedway in 1988.*

Below: *the Penske team holding the front row of the grid in 1988, with Rick Mears in pole position in car number 5.*

Bill Vukovich x 2
Indy's father-and-son dynasty

ILL VUKOVICH HOLDS THE INDIANAPOLIS ONE-LAP qualifying record for 1952. Bill Vukovich also holds the Indianapolis one-lap qualifying record for 1972. A remarkably long career, running at the front of the field? Not exactly.

For Bill Vukovich Senior and Junior are the only father and son to have set a one-lap qualifying record at Indianapolis. In 1952, Vukovich Senior set a one-lap record of 224.386 km/h (139.427 mph), driving the Howard Keck Fuel Injection Special, powered by a 270 cubic inch Offenhauser engine. Twenty years later, his son set a one-lap qualifying speed of 299.257 km/h (185.950 mph), this time driving an Eagle Offenhauser.

Vukovich Senior in many ways is the more remarkable. He also set a four-lap qualifying record in 1952 of 222.430 km/h (138.212 mph), but unfortunately managed to complete only 191 laps of the race. In 1953, however, he won the Indy 500, and he repeated that feat the following year as well! In 1955, Vukovich set the fastest four-lap qualifying time again, this time driving the Lindsay Hopkins Special, which lapped at 227.031 km/h (141.071 mph). The same year he also held the single qualifying lap record of 141.309 seconds, but after only 57 laps, the 'Mad Russian' crashed to his death.

Vukovich the elder was actually on course to win the epic 1952 Indianapolis 500, having led the race at record speed, but he spun off while leading, allowing Troy Ruttman's Agajanian Special (which was also Offenhauser-powered) to cart off the spoils.

'Billy' Vukovich Junior (as nicknamed by contemporary reports) started his 1972 Indianapolis 500 from the sixth row with his Eagle-Offenhauser, in the company of none other than A. J. Foyt. It was quite a remarkable year for qualifying, as the average speed of the grid was up 11.99 seconds from the previous year's grid – way more than normal. This was partly due to aerodynamic changes, which increased speeds but also stability. 'I feel safer this year at 195 than I did last year at 175,' explained Bobby Unser.

It was all to come to very little for 'Billy' however, on 27 May, as he retired in the early stages of the race with mechanical failure. Mark Donohue won the race, after a careful drive which had seen him hang back in third up to more or less the last minute. First, his team-mate Gary Bettenhausen, who had been leading for more than half the race, dropped out with engine trouble, and then the new leader, Jerry Grant, was forced to change a hopelessly unbalanced wheel. The net result was to donate the lead to Donohue.

All that makes little difference to the achievement of the Vukoviches. Their achievement was, in the words of Pete Lyons, reporting on the qualification sessions for *Autosport,* 'a singular event'. With the Andrettis and Villeneuves perhaps we are more used now to the idea of motor-racing dynasties, but we should not lose sight of the fact that the Vukoviches did it first.

Opposite: Bill Vukovich Senior before the 1955 Indianapolis in which he crashed and was fatally injured.

Below: the Vukoviches – the first in an ever-growing line of Indianapolis racing dynasties – held the one-lap qualifying records for races 20 years apart.

Land 5 Speed Records

Does it matter if Craig Breedlove beats us? Even if he took all his friends to the top of Everest and had a massive dinner party, when he gets there he'll still find the Union flag flying there at the top, because we were there first.

Andy Green, first man to drive through the sound barrier

The first records
Chasseloup-Laubat versus the 'Red Devil', 1898

THE LAND SPEED RECORD WAS OFFICIALLY INAUGURATED ON 18 DECEMBER 1898, WHEN THE FRENCHMAN COUNT GASTON DE CHASSELOUP-LAUBAT DROVE HIS JEANTAUD ELECTRIC CAR THROUGH AN OFFICIALLY TIMED FLYING KILOMETRE AT A SPEED OF 63.15 KM/H (39.24 MPH).

The Automobile Club de France (ACF) had held a timed hill climb at Chanteloup, 32 km (20 miles) from Paris, in late November. After performing well there but being beaten by a Belgian called Camille Jenatzy, Chasseloup-Laubat had used his status as a founder member of the ACF to make a secret request for it to stage a speed contest over a 2 km (1.2 mile) course in the Achères park in St Germain, Paris. There he became history's first land speed record-setter in his 1400 kg (3204 lb) contender, which generated 36 hp from its single electric motor.

Jenatzy had not been able to attend the contest, but the two met again at Achères on 17 January 1899, when the Belgian calmly registered a new record of 66.65 km/h (41.42 mph) in his own electric contender, which bore his name. Much was at stake, however, for Jeantaud had the commercial imperative of a monopoly on the French taxi market; Chasseloup-Laubat's immediate response was another new record of 70.31 km/h (43.69 mph). Within 10 days Jenatzy had bettered that with 80.33 km/h (49.92 mph), but Chasseloup-Laubat's fresh challenge met with mechanical and poor weather, factors that would frequently feature on record attempts.

Chasseloup-Laubat tried again on 4 March, and this time the Jeantaud bore the first signs of streamlining as a pointed nose improved its aerodynamics dramatically. He regained his honour as the fastest man on earth with 92.69 km/h (57.60 mph).

Jenatzy's nickname was 'The Red Devil', and he did not accept defeat easily. At the Compagnie Internationale des Transports Automobiles Electriques Jenatzy, in Paris, he set about creating the first car ever to be built specifically to break the land speed record. With a special alloy bodyshell designed and built by Carrosserie Rothschild, the vehicle resembled a torpedo on wheels. Two small electric motors were mounted on the rear axle, and generated more than 50 hp. Jenatzy called his new creation La Jamais Contente ('The Never Satisfied'), a name that somehow would come to encapsulate the spirit behind all such record-contenders. With its minimal resistance to the wind it was faster still. On 1 April 1899, Jenatzy sped through the measured kilometre at Achères at high speed, only to discover that the timekeepers had not been ready for him. Disappointed, he withdrew temporarily but returned on 29 April and attained a remarkable 105.87 km/h (65.79 mph), to regain the laurels and record the first occasions on which man had travelled at a mile a minute and had breached the 100 km/h barrier.

Chasseloup-Laubat did not respond, and thus ended the first great duel for land speed record honours.

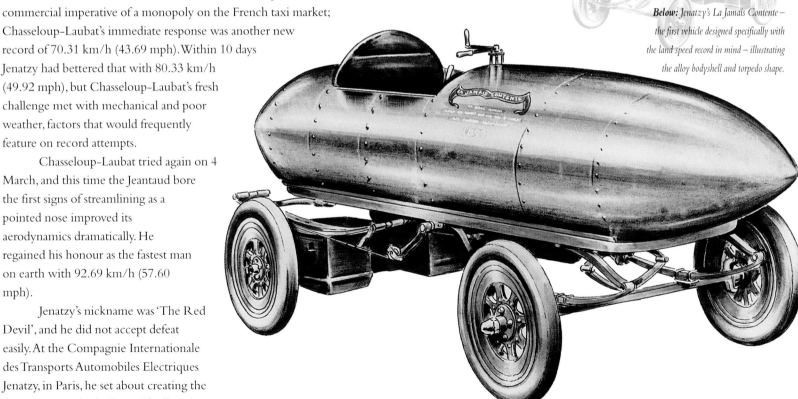

Overleaf: ThrustSSC, *holder of the land speed record which was achieved in October 1997 (see page 113).*

Below: Jenatzy's La Jamais Contente – *the first vehicle designed specifically with the land speed record in mind – illustrating the alloy bodyshell and torpedo shape.*

The success of steam
Léon Serpollet and the Oeuf des Pâques, 1902

N THE VERY EARLY DAYS OF THE LAND SPEED RECORD THE STEAM CAR WAS ONE OF THE MOST POTENT THREATS.

Count Gaston de Chasseloup-Laubat and Camille Jenatzy had staged the duel that established the first records in their electric cars, but in 1901 Frenchman Léon Serpollet completed a remarkable vehicle on which he had been working in secret for some time. Like many racing enthusiasts, he had started out with a minimal capital base, but had begged assistance and support from a number of well-wishers. The steam engine of his car had four cylinders and produced 106 bhp at only 1220 rpm, but required at least 20 minutes before it could generate a sufficient head of steam.

A degree of confusion still surrounds the precise identity of the car in which Serpollet subsequently set his records. Between 1901 and 1903 he built three steamers, two of them dumpy, relatively short vehicles which quite appositely reflected their unusual name: Oeuf des Pâques ('Easter Egg'). The third was longer and more like an upturned boat in shape, with a sleeker, chisel-like profile. Some contemporary sources suggest that the first record was established in one of the dumpy machines, but Serpollet's own publicity material used an illustration of the third car, and it seems more likely that this was indeed the one that he drove into the history books. Whatever the case, his success was firm indication at the time of the potential of steam's efficiency.

Serpollet went to the annual 'Speed Week' held on the Promenade des Anglais in Nice, which to this day remains a fast, straight – but markedly more populated – stretch of road on the sea-front of the fashionable French resort. His appearance created a great deal of local excitement, but there was also a strong body of opinion that such feats had little recognizable purpose. Some still even doubted the driver's ability to breathe at the speeds envisaged.

Serpollet ignored all this, and his car ran very well to defeat all of its petrol-powered rivals. When he came within 5 km/h (3 mph) of Jenatzy's three-year-old record of 105.87 km/h (65.79 mph), he was sufficiently encouraged to plan an all-out attack. A modified Oeuf des Pâques appeared in Nice the following April, and with little fuss Serpollet steamed through the measured kilometre in 29.8 seconds, the first time any man had ever travelled such a distance in less than half a minute. His average speed of 120.79 km/h (75.06 mph) beat Jenatzy's record comfortably.

It was a fabulous effort that underlined the advantages then offered by steam power, although ultimately it was a form of vehicle motivation that failed to catch on. It was not, however, the last fling for steam, as Fred Marriott would later achieve a startling 195.64 km/h (121.57 mph) when driving the Stanley brothers' steamer, Rocket, at Daytona Beach four years later.

Léon Serpollet on his record steam car at the annual 'Speed Week' show on the Promenade des Anglais in Nice.

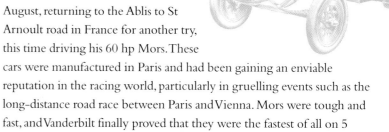

Petrol to the fore
The arrival of the internal combustion engine, 1902

ÉON SERPOLLET'S LAND SPEED RECORD OF 120.79 KM/H (75.06 MPH) WITH HIS STEAM CAR OEUF DES PÂQUES WAS A REMARKABLE ACHIEVEMENT THAT WRESTED THE ADVANTAGE AWAY FROM THE ELECTRIC CAR. But even as the Frenchman set his new mark on 13 April 1902, petrol-driven racing cars were already preparing to stake their own claim.

The first to try was an Englishman, the Hon. Charles Rolls (whose partnership with Henry Royce would come to epitomize the best in mechanical engineering via their Rolls-Royce concern). Rolls, too, went to Achères in April 1902, driving one of the four-cylinder, 9.2-litre Mors petrol-driven racing cars of the day, which developed 60 hp. His best speed, however, was 101.54 km/h (63.10 mph). Next came the millionaire American amateur racer, William K. Vanderbilt, Jr, who had equalled – but not beaten – Jenatzy's record in a petrol-driven Mercedes-Simplex 40 just before Serpollet's success. Later in April he tried again on the road between Chartres and Bonneval, and again between Ablis and St Arnoult, but on each occasion he came up short.

Incredibly, another Belgian, Baron Pierre de Caters, also matched Serpollet's record in a Mors in a speed trial outside Bruges in July. Activity in the record-breaking field was high, but drivers had to beat, not merely equal, a mark before they could claim a new one.

Vanderbilt was back in action in August, returning to the Ablis to St Arnoult road in France for another try, this time driving his 60 hp Mors. These cars were manufactured in Paris and had been gaining an enviable reputation in the racing world, particularly in gruelling events such as the long-distance road race between Paris and Vienna. Mors were tough and fast, and Vanderbilt finally proved that they were the fastest of all on 5 August 1902 when, by the smallest of margins, he beat Serpollet's mark with a speed of 122.43 km/h (76.08 mph).

For Vanderbilt it was the climax to a string of frustrating outings and justification for perseverance, but it was only the start for Mors. Just three months later the French racing driver Henri Fournier achieved 123.27 km/h (76.60 mph) in another Mors at Dourdan, and then 12 days later he was deposed by fellow Frenchman Augières whose Mors went through the kilometre at 124.12 km/h (77.13 mph).

Each of the speed increments had been minimal, and the timing of the day lacked the sophistication of later years. Eventually the Association Internationale des Automobile Clubs Reconnus (AIACR), which took over timekeeping from the ACF, would insist that each new record had to exceed the old by one per cent, which cleared up a great deal of confusion and argument. For now, however, petrol was in firm control. Electricity had had its day, and steam had but one more shout in 1906 as the internal combustion engine prepared to enjoy a lengthy period of complete domination.

The Hon. Charles Rolls at the wheel of one of his four-cylinder Mors car in 1902, which marked the arrival of the internal combustion engine.

The first to 100 mph
Edging closer to the magic ton …, 1904

THE CELEBRATED DR JOHNSON HAD ONCE MEMORABLY REMARKED TO HIS ASSOCIATE, JAMES BOSWELL: 'FIE, SIR – TWENTY MILES IN ONE HOUR UPON A COACH? No man could rush so fast through the air and continue to draw breath!'

But man had indeed survived speeds far higher than that, and as Augières achieved his new record of 124.12 km/h (77.13 mph) at Dourdan on 17 November 1902 thoughts inevitably began to focus on the next big figure: 160 km (100 miles) in one hour.

Since Serpollet's 16 km/h (10 mph) jump over Jenatzy's last record, speeds had risen fractionally, but the new target came closer in 1903 when another French car manufacturer, Gobron-Brillié, stepped into the ring. The company was based, like Mors, in Paris, and specialized in building big, strong cars powered by advanced, horizontally opposed, four-cylinder engines, which produced 110 hp from 13.5 litres.

On 17 July 1903 the Belgian racing driver Arthur Duray took one of the specially streamlined cars to a speed meeting on the Nieuport road just outside Ostend, and there he raised Augières's record to 134.32 km/h (83.47 mph). This was actually beaten shortly afterwards by the Hon. Charles Rolls whose Mors was timed at 136.35 km/h (84.73 mph) on the Duke of Portland's estate at Clipstone, England, but the ACF refused to ratify the timing equipment used by the Automobile Club of Great Britain and Ireland (ACGBI, the forerunner of the RAC). Four months later Duray went to Dourdan, and there he edged his record up to the same speed that Rolls had achieved, 136.35 km/h (84.73 mph).

1904 brought another rash of attempts as the popularity of record-breaking soared. Henry Ford and William K. Vanderbilt both claimed to have set new records in excess of 145 km/h (90 mph) on American soil, the former on the frozen Lake St Clair with his Ford Arrow, the latter at Daytona Beach in his Mercedes 90. But yet again neither was recognized by European authorities because the ACF did not approve of the equipment that the American Automobile Association (AAA) chose to use. Instead, it fell to racing driver Louis Rigolly to take his Gobron-Brillié to Nice where, on 31 March, he achieved 152.52 km/h (94.78 mph). That lasted until May, when Baron Pierre de Caters made up for his disappointment in only equalling Jenatzy's old record in 1902 by setting a new record of 156.50 km/h (97.25 mph) in his Mercedes at Ostend. The 160 km/h (100 mph) mark could now only be a matter of months away.

Sure enough, on 21 July Rigolly also went to Ostend, and there he pushed his Gobron-Brillié through the kilometre at 166.64 km/h (103.55 mph), to claim yet another of the sport's milestone records. This was the age when racing cars could break the land speed record; a week after his triumph Rigolly finished fourth in the Gobron in the Circuit des Ardennes. But the day of the pure land speed special was fast approaching.

Blitzen Benz
Reshaping the future, 1909

FRED MARRIOTT'S STARTLING PERFORMANCE IN THE STANLEY STEAMER HAD ERASED VICTOR HEMERY'S RECORD OF 176.46 KM/H (109.65 MPH) AND ELEVATED IT TO 195.64 KM/H (121.57 MPH) IN 1906, BUT IN 1909 THE BENZ COMPANY IN GERMANY CREATED

a formidable new challenger that would come to be known as the Blitzen ('lightning') Benz, and which would reshape the future.

The engine had eight large cylinders and a cubic capacity of 21,500 cc, and developed 200 hp at 1600 rpm. This was transmitted via the usual chains to the rear wheels, and the car was notable for the sleekness of its contours. The bodyshell was very slim, with a peaked radiator shroud and a pointed, upswept tail, and its lines were the contemporary embodiment of speed.

The Benz participated successfully in races in Germany before being sent to the newly opened Brooklands banked track in 1909. The French

driver Victor Hemery made several runs before clocking a speed of 202.69 km/h (125.95 mph), which was ratified as a new record.

While the Benz was on display in the company's showrooms in New York, it was purchased by showman and racing driver Barney Oldfield, a colourful opportunist whose trademark was to race chewing on an unlit cigar. Oldfield took the car to Daytona Beach in Florida in March 1910, and though the timing apparatus was not ratified by the European authority, the Association Internationale des Automobile Clubs Reconnus (AIACR) in France, he claimed a new speed record of 211.26 km/h (131.27 mph) and proclaimed himself the fastest man on earth. Just over a year later, after the Benz had been subjected to a season of dirt-track racing across America, another American racer, Wild Bob Burman, used the car to claim another unofficial record at Daytona. He said that he had attained 227.50 km/h (141.37 mph).

Three years later an Englishman, Major L.G. Hornsted, took a Blitzen Benz back to Brooklands in June 1914, shortly before the outbreak of the

The Blitzen Benz was characterized by an unusually streamlined, thin body and peaked radiator shroud.

First World War. By now the Royal Automobile Club (RAC) in Britain and France's AIACR had agreed that records should be based on the mean times taken for two runs, in opposing directions, made within an hour of one another, to even out the vagaries of strong wind or favourable gradient. This was another reason why Burman's record had never been accepted.

Building up as much speed as possible by racing round the bankings before emerging into the measured distance, Hornsted recorded 206.24 km/h (128.16 mph) in one direction and 193.48 km/h (120.23 mph) in the other, to create the first two-way land speed record of 199.71 km/h (124.10 mph).

Though this did not actually better Hemery's original Brooklands figure, it was accepted by the AIACR as the new mark because it conformed to the newly introduced regulation. In any case, Hornsted's one-way best did beat Hemery's figure.

Today, the Daimler-Benz Museum in Stuttgart-Untertürkheim has on display a very well restored Blitzen Benz, together with Daimler-Benz's stillborn T80 land speed record-contender of 1939.

Guinness is good for you
The arrival of the aero-engined car, 1922

THE FIRST WORLD WAR BEQUEATHED AN UNUSUAL LEGACY TO THE WORLD OF MOTOR SPORT: THE AERO-ENGINE. AND IT WAS THE SUNBEAM MOTOR COMPANY, based in Wolverhampton, that would in 1922 usher in the era of the aero-engined record car, which has persisted to this day.

Sunbeam had an enviable reputation in motor racing, and after hostilities had ceased in 1918 it was not long before the imaginative chief designer, Louis Coatalen, conceived the idea of mounting one of the company's wartime 18,300 cc Manitou V12 engines into a racing-car chassis. The result was what became known as the 350 hp Sunbeam, which was completed in 1920. It competed in several races and hill climbs, often with distinction, but one of its greatest moments came on 17 May 1922 when Kenelm Lee Guinness, founder of the well-known KLG spark-plug company, used it to smash Hornsted's land speed record.

Like the Major, Guinness took the Sunbeam to Brooklands, after first taking great trouble to ensure that the pernickety AIACR would recognize any performance by approving the British timekeeping. The result was a new record of 215.24 km/h (133.75 mph), to Coatalen's great delight.

Coatalen was eventually persuaded to sell this remarkable car to Captain Malcolm Campbell, and Sunbeam's next record-contender was a very different machine. This time Coatalen opted for something much more

scientific and less brutal when he combined two obsolete Sunbeam two-litre Grand Prix engines to create a four-litre V12 which produced 306 supercharged horsepower. The car weighed only 914 kg (2016 lb), and was handled by Britain's great motor sport star, Major Henry Segrave, the winner of the 1923 French GP. On Southport Sands on 16 March 1926 he erased Malcolm Campbell's hard-won record with the 350 hp Sunbeam Bluebird with a speed of 245.15 km/h (152.33 mph) despite serious problems with fractured supercharger casings.

The next project came at Segrave's behest, and Coatalen reverted to his previous philosophy as he created the 1000 hp Sunbeam. This monster had two 22,500 cc Sunbeam Matabele V12 aero-engines, one mounted ahead of the driver, the other behind. It was designed to smash the 320 km/h (200 mph) barrier at a time when Campbell and Thomas were fighting towards 290 (180), and its body resembled an upturned boat which enclosed all four wheels.

While Segrave was bound for Daytona he heard the news of Parry Thomas's death at Pendine, but resolved to carry on. And on 29 March he became the first man to travel at 320 km/h (200 mph) on land when he achieved 327.95 km/h (203.792 mph), even though he had skidded wildly at maximum speed and then been forced to steer into the sea on the first run as his brakes overheated.

Sunbeam's last challenger, the Silver Bullet in 1930, sadly proved a flop, plagued by financial and mechanical problems in Kaye Don's hands.

Today, the 350 hp Sunbeam and the 1000 hp Sunbeam are both on display at the National Motor Museum, Beaulieu. The four-litre V12 is in private hands.

Tribute to a hero
Parry Thomas and Babs, 1927

WHILE HIS BROOKLANDS RACE TRACK RIVAL MALCOLM CAMPBELL WAS SAID TO HAVE SPENT £10,000 DEVELOPING HIS BLUEBIRD LAND SPEED RECORD CAR, John Godfrey Parry Thomas paid the estate of the late Count Zborowski a mere £125 for the car known as the Higham Special. Its crudeness was at odds with Thomas's engineering genius, but though he had developed his own racing cars for Brooklands, he could not afford to build his own record-contender and instead saw potential in Zborowski's old car.

Its heart was a 26,900 cc, 400 hp, prewar Liberty aero-engine which drove the rear wheels via chains. Thomas knew that if he brought his engineering talents to bear the car could break the record, which was held by Major Henry Segrave at 245.15 km/h (152.33 mph).

Thomas lowered the chassis, modified the engine and the clutch and manufactured a sleeker bodyshell with better aerodynamics. When the work was finished, he painted the car white with blue chassis side members and christened it Babs.

In 1925 the quiet-spoken Welshman, who liked to race wearing a Fair Isle sweater, took Babs to the beach at Pendine Sands in north Wales, but was beaten by poor weather. After prolonged tests at Brooklands he again moved to Pendine in April 1926. On the 27th Babs roared precariously down the beach, swaying from side to side as its engine belched black clouds of smoke. In two runs Thomas achieved his goal, becoming the fastest man on earth with an average speed of 272.45 km/h (169.30 mph).

He believed that Babs could do better, however, for the engine had not been running properly. He worked all night in his garage at the Beach Hotel to cure misfiring, and tried again the following day. Though the engine was still faltering, Babs was in better form and he broke his own record with a speed of 275.22 km/h (171.02 mph).

Despite the dramatic increase over Segrave's old record, Thomas knew Babs could go faster still, and set about developing it further as Campbell and Segrave prepared new contenders. Segrave's twin-engined Sunbeam was the more fearsome, and while that car was on its way to Daytona Beach, where Segrave would make his attempt at 320 km/h (200 mph), Thomas went back to Pendine with Babs now looking even sleeker. On 1 March 1927 he set up camp again at the Beach Hotel, but endured poor weather and mechanical problems which prevented runs at more than 273 kmh (170 mph). Then, on 3 March, while travelling at an estimated speed of 290 km/h (180 mph), Babs overturned, killing him instantly. The men who buried the giant car there in the sand suggested either that a driving chain had snapped or that a wheel had collapsed. Poor Thomas became the first man ever to die trying to break the land speed record.

In 1969 Welsh engineer Owen Wyn Owen exhumed Babs, and today the big white car has been restored as a moving tribute to a long-departed hero.

'Babs' after the accident at Pendine which killed her driver Parry Thomas in 1927.

The Bluebird of happiness
Malcolm Campbell and his immortal machine, 1931

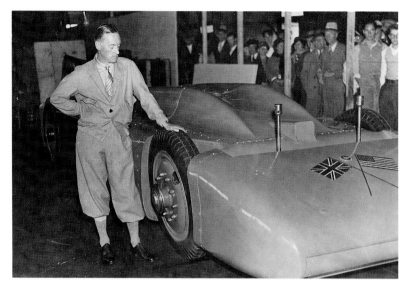

N O MAN EVER COVETED THE LAND SPEED RECORD AS MUCH AS CAPTAIN (LATER SIR) MALCOLM CAMPBELL. HAVING SEEN HOW KENELM LEE GUINNESS SUCCEEDED IN SQUEEZING MORE THAN 209 KM/H (130 MPH) OUT OF THE 350 HP SUNBEAM AT BROOKLANDS IN 1922, Campbell set his heart on acquiring the car from Sunbeam designer, Louis Coatalen. Eventually his browbeating paid off. Having painted it in his traditional Bluebird blue, Campbell twice smashed the record, only to have each disallowed on technicalities.

Some might have given up, but each disappointment only made Campbell more determined. Working with his faithful mechanic, Leo Villa, he instigated further modifications and tried again at Pendine Sands in September 1924. By now he was aiming for Ernest Eldridge's new record of 234.97 km/h (146.01 mph), and he succeeded, recording 235.15 km/h (146.16 mph) at a time when there had yet to be an official requirement for new records to exceed old by one per cent. The following year he became the first to 241 km/h (150 mph), again with the Sunbeam.

By the time Segrave, with the four-litre Sunbeam, and Parry Thomas with Babs had beaten that, Campbell was already working on a bespoke Bluebird, with a 23,900 cc Napier Lion aero-engine loaned by the Air

One of the most famous figures in land speed history, Sir Malcolm Campbell, and his Bluebird racers, in which he consistently strove to exceed the records.

Ministry. In various guises this was to be the car that would take him to four miles a minute and a knighthood. In 1927 at Pendine he reached 281.439 km/h (174.883 mph). In February 1928, with Bluebird much modified, he claimed 333.054 km/h (206.956 mph). He suffered failure in 1929 at Verneuk Pan in South Africa, as Segrave took his record away, but the new version of Bluebird for 1931 boosted him to 396.032 km/h (246.09 mph) on his return to Daytona, and that knighthood. He went back again in February 1932, upping his speed to 408.713 km/h (253.97 mph).

Campbell, however, was never satisfied. Like Camille Jenatzy, he always wanted more. The Napier Lion gave way to the more powerful V12 Rolls-Royce R engine for 1933, and the otherwise similar Bluebird clocked 438.469 km/h (272.46 mph) at Daytona, again in February. Then the gifted Reid Railton redesigned the car yet again, with an even sleeker bodyshell and twin rear wheels in an effort to improve traction. Thus, when all the effort and investment allowed him to increase his record by only 6 km/h (4 mph) at Daytona in March 1935, Campbell was bitterly disappointed.

He switched to the Bonneville Salt Flats in Utah that September, and there, on a significantly harder surface which provoked much less wheelspin, he pushed the record to 484.606 km/h (301.129 mph). It was his last great feat on wheels before he switched to the water speed record.

Twenty-five years after his father's last land record, Donald Campbell survived the crash of his own Bluebird-Proteus at Bonneville, in September 1960. In July 1964 he finally succeeded in breaking the official land speed record, with a speed of 648.708 km/h (403.1 mph) on Lake Eyre in the Australian outback.

Thunderbolt versus Railton Special
Battle of the British, 1938

IR MALCOLM CAMPBELL HAD RETIRED TO CONCENTRATE ON THE WATER SPEED RECORD WHEN TWO MORE ENGLISHMEN STEPPED FORWARD TO CHALLENGE HIS 484.606 KM/H (301.129 MPH) BENCHMARK.

George Eyston was a tall, quiet-spoken man who preferred action to words. He was a successful racing driver who had already taken many class and endurance records in smaller cars, and had been a good friend of former record-holder Ernest Eldridge. The creation of a land speed record car was a logical progression and, like Camille Jenatzy, he set about designing his own. Campbell's final Bluebird had used a single Rolls-Royce R V12 engine; Eyston used two, mounted side-by-side amidships. There were four steered wheels at the front and, like Bluebird, the mammoth Thunderbolt used twin rear wheels to transmit the 4700 bhp generated by its combined capacity of 73,000 cc.

While the finishing touches were being put to Thunderbolt at the Bean car factory in Staffordshire in the middle of 1937, Eyston's old friend and Brooklands rival, John Cobb, was beginning to consider his own record car. Like Eyston, Cobb was a big man who hated the limelight and let his achievements speak for themselves. He commissioned the brilliant

designer Reid Railton, who had worked with Campbell, to create a car capable of more than 563 km/h (350 mph). Cobb could obtain only Napier Lion engines, but Railton laid them out cleverly in an S-shaped backbone chassis, each engine driving an axle in the record's first application of four-wheel drive.

Eyston went to Bonneville, the scene of many of his successful endurance records, in October 1937. It was a tribute to his ability as a designer that Thunderbolt performed with remarkable reliability, and after a wait for the right weather conditions he achieved 502.10 km/h (312.00 mph) on 19 November.

Cobb's Railton Special was ready for 1938, when the two shared the salt. On 27 August Eyston increased his own record to 556.01 km/h (345.50 mph) before Cobb retaliated with 563.57 km/h (350.20 mph) on 15 September. But Eyston had the final say for the year when, less than 24 hours later, he regained the honours with a speed of 575.32 km/h (357.50 mph).

A remarkable fellow, Eyston had already achieved a significantly faster speed only to discover that timekeeper Art Pillsbury's equipment had malfunctioned. Eyston simply put his arm round the distraught Pillsbury and told the expectant media that he had just been on a test run. Later still, he would walk calmly away after the rear suspension had failed at a speed well over his final record.

Cobb returned alone in 1939 to record 594.95 km/h (369.70 mph). After the Second World War he returned to the salt and became the first man ever to travel faster than 643 km/h (400 mph) on one run, which cemented his third and final record at 634.38 km/h (394.20 mph).

Throughout their remarkable duel, Eyston and Cobb retained their friendship and sense of sportsmanship.

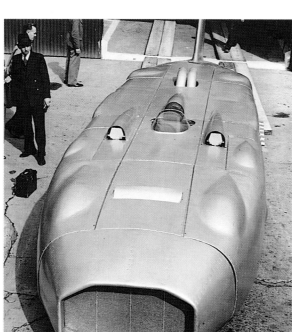

Above left: *Campbell's Bluebird.*

Above right: *John Cobb with his twin-engined Railton Special.*

Left: *Eyston's mammoth car Thunderbolt.*

'For my next trick'
Breedlove's Spirit of America, 1963

CRAIG BREEDLOVE'S SPIRIT OF AMERICA WAS NOT THE FIRST CAR TO ABANDON CONVENTIONAL TRANSMISSION AND RELY ON THE PURE THRUST OF A TURBOJET AERO-ENGINE BUT IT WAS THE FIRST TO SUCCEED.

The Sixties heralded an explosion of speed. First, Californian physician Dr Nathan Ostich ran his jet-propelled Flying Caduceus at Bonneville, but mechanical problems prevented him from bettering 532 km/h (331 mph).

Internationale de l'Automobile (FIA) said that the record was not official because there was no category for jetcars. Therefore the record could not be ratified. But the Fédération International Motocyclisme (FIM) said that it would accept it because, with its three wheels, Spirit of America qualified as a motorcycle and sidecar! Later, the FIA recognized a separate category for jetcars, and Tom Green achieved 664.96 km/h (413.20 mph) on 2 October 1964, to set the first official jet record. Three days later Art Arfons took his jet-powered Green Monster to 698.46 km/h (434.02 mph).

Breedlove was ready again on 13 October, and propelled his car to his first official record with an average speed of 754.31 km/h (468.72 mph). But he knew that he could do better still, and two days later he went

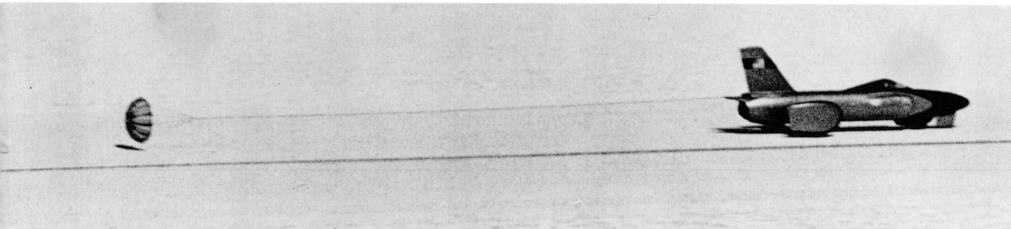

The Spirit of America being slowed down by parachute after breaking the world land speed record at the Bonneville Salt Flats in 1963.

Breedlove largely designed and built his car himself, and it was ready by 1962. It had only one front wheel and two at the back, mounted far apart for maximum stability. This extraordinary tricycle resembled a fighter aeroplane without wings, and was powered by a General Electric J47 engine, which produced 2358 kg (5200 lb) of thrust, or the equivalent of 10,000 hp. Without the need for a complicated gearbox to transmit all that power to the wheels, Spirit of America was literally blown along by the exhaust gases. Breedlove did not have to worry about traditional problems such as wheelspin.

That year he was obliged to withdraw after problems steering the car in a straight line had hampered his test runs at Bonneville. And as he made his way back to California he heard the news that rival Glenn Leasher had been killed when his Infinity jetcar crashed on the salt.

Like Segrave, Breedlove resolved to continue. He returned to Bonneville and on 5 August 1963, while Donald Campbell and the wheel-driven Bluebird were suffering the poor weather on Australia's Lake Eyre, Breedlove flashed to 655.70 km/h (407.45 mph). In Paris the Fédération

significantly faster on his first run. On the return, however, both braking parachutes tore away, and when he tried to slow down with the wheel brakes they melted at 643 km/h (400 mph). Brakeless, Breedlove careered down the salt, razored down a telegraph pole and had to swim for his life when Spirit of America dived over a bank and into a brine pond. He broke his car, but he also broke the record, with 846.94 km/h (526.28 mph), marking the first time man had travelled over 800 km/h (500 mph) on land.

As he clambered to safety, Breedlove joked: 'For my next trick, I'll set myself afire!'

Art Arfons
The junkyard genius, 1964

THEY CALLED HIM THE JUNKYARD GENIUS OF THE JET SET, AND CERTAINLY ART ARFONS OF AKRON, OHIO, HAD A REMARKABLE WAY WITH MACHINERY. He had been drag racing for years when, in 1963, he really started to get serious about going very fast at Bonneville. He bought a General Electric J79 turbojet engine at a disposal sale, paying next to nothing for it because somebody had accidentally rammed a spike down the intake. The turbine blades were damaged and the unit was deemed unserviceable. When Arfons approached GE for a maintenance manual he was told he could not have one; later representatives of the military tried to get him to give the engine back. But Arfons ploughed on and astounded them all by rebuilding it despite his lack of experience.

He installed it in a car he built himself, with the help of long-time associate Ed Snyder. He located a cockpit either side of the giant engine, fashioned a crude bodyshell, and headed off to Bonneville. The most expensive things about the vehicle, which in line with his past traditions he called Green Monster, were the wheels and tyres he had persuaded Firestone to supply. The rest of the car cost him little more than $10,000.

Green Monster was a devastatingly efficient car. Within days of arriving at Bonneville in October 1964, Arfons went loping down the salt at 698.46 km/h (434.02 mph). It was a new land speed record, and erased the mark set only three days earlier by Tom Green, whose Wingfoot Express was the property of Art's estranged brother, Walt. His success did not improve their relationship.

After arch-rival Craig Breedlove had raised the record twice before damaging his Spirit of America, Arfons went out again for the final say of that dramatic 1964 season. And with his customary lack of fuss he beat Breedlove by registering 863.72 km/h (536.71 mph).

They met again at Bonneville the following year, Arfons with an improved Green Monster, Breedlove with a brand new car called Spirit of America – Sonic 1. And though Breedlove broke Arfons's record with a speed of 893.93 km/h (555.48 mph) on 2 November, five days later Arfons regained it when he powered the Monster to 927.84 km/h (576.55 mph). But this time it was Breedlove's turn to have the last word, as he ran again a week later and raised the record to 966.54 km/h (600.601 mph).

The season ended as the weather deteriorated, but Arfons came back alone the following November, when the salt was back in good condition. Intent on regaining the record, he was travelling over 965 km/h (600 mph) when a wheel bearing seized and pitched the Monster into a horrifying series of rolls. To the amazement of onlookers, Arfons survived the terrible battering with nothing worse than bruising and cuts.

Years later, into his sixties, he was still active at Bonneville with a smaller Green Monster. Once a racer, always a racer.

Art Arfons with his Green Monster after their record-breaking run at Bonneville in October 1964.

Spirit of America –
Sonic 1 and Sonic Arrow
Supersonic coke bottle and garden roller, 1965 and 1996

'T'HE PLAN WAS TO GO SUPERSONIC IN 1965, BUT IT WOULD BE 30 MORE YEARS BEFORE CRAIG BREEDLOVE COULD REALLY START TO WORK CLOSE TO SUCH SPEEDS.

When he rolled out Spirit of America – Sonic 1 at the beginning of 1965, the Goodyear-sponsored car was a surprise for rival Art Arfons, who had won the record championship of 1964 after Breedlove's wild ride into a brine lake in the original three-wheeled Spirit of America.

Without further ado, Breedlove and his team had set to work on the new car which, like Arfons's Green Monster, would be powered by a General Electric J79 turbojet capable of producing 6800 kg (15,000 lb) of thrust. It was a very different machine, which in plain view had the appearance of a coke bottle as part of Breedlove's rule-of-thumb aerodynamics, for this time the plan was to create something really special: the first supersonic car.

The first time out at Bonneville in 1965, the Spirit quickly recaptured its lost record, with 893.93 km/h (555.48 mph), but there was evidence of front-end lift which Breedlove countered by modifying the bodywork. Arfons took the record away five days later, but eight days later still Breedlove became the first man to hit 965 km/h (600 mph), with his fifth record, at 966.54 km/h (600.601 mph). Again, however, there had been signs of dangerous front-end lift which threatened to flip the car over backwards. Breedlove retired, to rest on his well-earned laurels.

Then, 25 years later, he told Richard Noble that he intended not just to challenge Thrust 2's record, but to build a supersonic car. Thus was born Spirit of America – Sonic Arrow, a 13 m (44 ft)-long projectile which again outrigged its two rear wheels but ran on no fewer than three front wheels, all mounted very close together. Breedlove jokingly called it his garden roller. With a General Electric J79 tweaked to 9072 kg (20,000 lb) of thrust, Breedlove was aiming for 1206 km/h (750 mph).

The car was ready by October 1996 and, after trials at Bonneville, Breedlove transferred to the Black Rock Desert in Nevada, where Noble had set his record with Thrust 2. Craig was travelling at a speed he later estimated to be 1086 km/h (675 mph) when a shockwave built up beneath one of the rear axle fairings and in an instant Spirit of America was speeding down the desert on its side before describing a three kilometre (two mile) circle and coming to rest. Breedlove was unharmed but understandably shaken, while the Spirit was remarkably little damaged. He went back to his

base in Rio Vista, and was ready for 1997 and the battle with ThrustSSC which he and Noble billed as the 'Race of the Century'. The British won the fight to go supersonic as Breedlove endured what he called a summer from hell, but he still dreams of being the first to reach 1287 km/h (800 mph).

Burning with a Blue Flame
Rocket-propulsion breaks the 1000 km/h barrier, 1970

THE BLUE FLAME WAS THE FIRST SUCCESSFUL ROCKET-PROPELLED CONTENDER AND THE FIRST FOR A VERY LONG TIME WHOSE CHASSIS AND ENGINE WERE DESIGNED SPECIFICALLY FOR THEIR TASK.

The project was the brainchild of two American drag-racing enthusiasts, Dick Keller and Ray Dausman. Their first move was to prove the concept by building a small-scale version of their engine. By 1964 that was working successfully, so they moved on to build a bigger version and installed it in a small dragster which they called the X-1 (after Chuck Yeager's supersonic plane). This again proved successful, and by 1965 they had been joined by dragster builder and racer Pete Farnsworth. Together they formed Reaction Dynamics in Milwaukee, Wisconsin. Their engine functioned by passing hydrogen peroxide over a catalyst mat of silver and nickel wire. This decomposed the hydrogen peroxide almost instantly into water and oxygen. The water thus became superheated steam and with the oxygen it passed at tremendous velocity through the rocket nozzle to produce fabulous power. Reaction Dynamics contracted with the American Institute of Gas Technology (IGT) to use its liquefied natural gas as a bi-propellant. With the LNG, they estimated a maximum of 9979 kg (22,000 lb) of thrust. The car was christened Blue Flame in deference to IGT's corporate symbol.

Blue Flame was 11.7 m (38 ft 6 in) long and looked like a long pencil on wheels, with the front pair housed within the cylindrical fuselage and the rears outrigged for roll stability. Like Breedlove's Spirit of America – Sonic 1, it was designed for supersonic speed.

When the intended driver, Chuck Suba, was killed in a drag-racing accident, Reaction Dynamics approached veteran drag racer

Don Garlits and Craig Breedlove. Both turned them down, but Breedlove suggested a former trainee astronaut, drag car and speedboat racer called Gary Gabelich.

The Blue Flame finally went to Bonneville in 1970, a year behind schedule, and initially Gabelich ran into considerable mechanical trouble as the catalyst mats kept burning out and seals in the hydrogen peroxide system proved fragile. On 18 October he ran one-way at a tantalizing 1000.22 km/h (621.53 mph) but could not make a return run after another seal failed.

With time, weather and finances in a precarious state, the Reaction Dynamics team regrouped for one final try, opting to push-start the Blue Flame to 56 km/h (35 mph) to ease the strain on the catalyst mats. On 23 October, Gabelich was strapped aboard, and made one run at 993.906 km/h (617.602 mph). But then it began to rain. Gabelich said: 'I saw the clouds part momentarily in the shape of the cross, so I knew the Man was with us.'

He just beat a downpour as he recorded the return run, when he recorded 1009.492 km/h (627.287 mph), and the record was his at 1001.639 km/h (622.407 mph), the first time anyone had broken the 1000 km/h barrier. And he had done it in the nick of time.

The custom-made, rocket-propelled Blue Flame, exhibiting its streamlined shape and immense speed capabilities at Bonneville where it broke the world record.

Budweiser Rocket
Controversy on wheels, 1979

THE LAND SPEED RECORD WAS NO STRANGER TO CONTROVERSY WHEN TIMING BODIES REFUSED TO RECOGNIZE ONE ANOTHER'S SYSTEMS. The French authority, the AIACR, was notorious for refusing to accept American figures, with the result that it declined to ratify records claimed to have been set on American soil. It was not until 1927, when Henry Segrave took his 1000 hp Sunbeam to Daytona, that the situation was consolidated as he used all his considerable charm to bring the disparate parties together. In 1979, however, the most controversial of all projects made an audacious claim to have breached the sound barrier on land.

Bill Fredrick was a Californian car builder whose Valkyrie jetcar had been driven at Bonneville by Gary Gabelich in 1962. By 1976 Fredrick had created a very slim rocket car, called the SMI Motivator, which was said to have reached speeds of more than 965 km/h (600 mph) at Bonneville in the hands of stuntman Hal Needham and stuntwoman Kitty O'Neil.

For 1979 Fredrick built another new rocket car, which was 11.8 m (39 ft) long, with a rear track of 3 m (10 ft) and a fuselage that was just over 51 cm (20 in) wide. Power came from a Romatec V4 rocket engine which produced 5896 kg (13,000 lb) of thrust on hydrogen peroxide. This time Fredrick hired stuntman Stan Barrett to drive the car, which would be sponsored by Budweiser. They took the car to Bonneville that year, where Fredrick announced that he had no time for the official regulations, which required two passes through a measured kilometre or mile, within one hour of each other. Instead, the Budweiser Rocket would be timed in only one direction over a 40 m (132 ft) trap.

The team transferred to Edwards Air Force Base in California after finding Bonneville's surface unsatisfactory. There, the car would be timed over a 16 m (52.8 ft) trap, and the United States Air Force would measure speed by radar. For greater power Fredrick had also incorporated a 2721 kg (6000 lb) thrust Sidewinder missile.

On 17 December 1979 Barrett made the most controversial run in the record's history. At first the highest speed that the radar picked up was 48 km/h (30 mph), as a water truck ambled across the desert. Later it was calculated that Barrett had reached 1190.344 km/h (739.666 mph), or Mach 1.0106. But Budweiser refused to pay a bonus because so many people doubted the achievement. It was not until Fredrick and Needham prevailed upon no less a figure than Chuck Yeager, the first man to fly at supersonic speed, to endorse the performance that they got their money.

Art Arfons, Craig Breedlove and Gary Gabelich resolutely refused to accept that the run had been supersonic. No sonic boom was ever heard in the vicinity and, as ThrustSSC would prove, cars travelling at such velocity most certainly produce them. Few actually knew what the Budweiser Rocket really achieved, only that it was certainly not official.

Hal Needham, Stan Barrett and Bill Fredrick with the Budweiser Rocket, the team that made the most controversial land speed run in 1979.

Thrust 2 and ThrustSSC
Dreams fulfilled, 1983 and 1997

RICHARD NOBLE ALWAYS HAD ASPIRATIONS OF SUPERSONIC SPEED LONG BEFORE HE HAD A CAR CAPABLE OF IT. The Briton decided to do something about his dream of breaking the land speed record when he built his own jet-powered car, Thrust 1, in 1974. When it was destroyed in an accident in March 1977 he sold the remains for scrap and invested the proceeds in its replacement, Thrust 2.

This was a very different project, run on wholly professional lines, with John Ackroyd as designer and Noble raising the money. It took them four years to finish off the car, which was a refined version of the Arfons Green Monster concept with a cockpit either side of a Rolls-Royce Avon engine from the Lightning fighter aircraft. Noble took it to Bonneville in 1981, but was forced to return to England by poor weather.

The following year's attempt was delayed after he damaged the car during a test run, and when Bonneville flooded he made an emergency relocation to the Black Rock Desert in Nevada. As winter closed in he reached a speed of 950.373 km/h (590.551 mph) before having to go home again. With sufficient money for a final attempt, he returned to Black Rock in September 1983, and on 4 October succeeded in breaking Gabelich's record with a speed of 1019.440 km/h (633.468 mph).

At Bonneville in 1990, Noble learned of Breedlove's supersonic plans, and remembered his own original plans for a similar car. He immediately decided: 'If he was going to do that, I wasn't going to let him do it without one hell of a battle.'

Aerodynamicist Ron Ayers created a dramatic new concept for Noble's new car, ThrustSSC (for Super Sonic Car). It would be powered by two Rolls-Royce Spey bypass jet engines each capable of producing 10,206 kg (22,500 lb) of thrust. These would be mounted far forward for maximum stability, which meant that the rear wheels would have to be steered. The highly unorthodox machine was finally completed in 1996, after the investment of 100,000 man-hours.

Noble had decided he could not drive and manage the project, so RAF Squadron Leader Andy Green was selected for the task. That year they tested on the Al Jafr desert in Jordan, reaching 532 km/h (331 mph). The following June Green reached 869 km/h (540 mph) there, before transferring to Black Rock. There, after the usual development problems, he smashed Thrust 2's record by the largest ever margin, establishing a new mark of 1149.271 km/h (714.144 mph) on 25 September. But that was only the beginning. The team kept building up speed until on 15 October 1997,

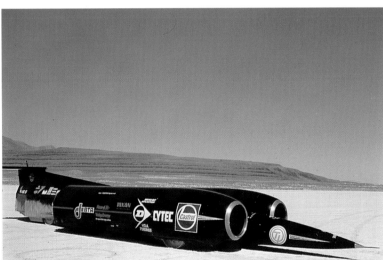

almost half a century to the day since Yeager's maiden supersonic flight, Green broke through the sound barrier to establish the first ever supersonic land speed record at 1227.952 km/h (763.035 mph).

On the eve of the record's centenary, it could not have been a more fitting climax to 100 years of the pursuit of speed on land.

Top left: Richard Noble with Thrust 2.

Bottom left: in action across the sands of the Black Rock Desert, Nevada.

Top right: Squadron Leader Andy Green, driver of the famous ThrustSSC in its world record breaking attempt.

Bottom right: ThrustSSC, holder of the land speed record which was achieved in October 1997.

Motorcycle Racing

6

*Over 300 mph on a motorcycle, you don't
even want to blink, let alone sneeze or shudder.*

Don Vesco, former world speed record–holder

And did those wheels, in ancient times . . . ?

Brooklands – the world's first purpose-built circuit, 1907

IN THE EARLY DAYS OF THE TWENTIETH CENTURY, WHEN MOTORCYCLE DESIGN WAS IN ITS INFANCY, RACING TOOK PLACE ON PUBLIC ROADS – not the smooth, fast roads we have today but dusty, rutted, potholed tracks that were more a test of the machines' robust construction than their outright speed.

Predictably, speed addicts soon clamoured for faster roads, and in 1907 the Brooklands circuit opened near Weybridge in Surrey – the world's first purpose-built motor-racing circuit. It was 4.43 km (2.75 miles) long, well-surfaced, and featured steep banking to help cars and bikes round the corners – crucial at a time when fearsome engines were being shoehorned into what were little more than bicycle frames.

In its heyday in the Twenties and Thirties, Brooklands was the world's favourite circuit, hosting races, record attempts and intensive testing by all the manufacturers. Its finest two-wheeled hour came in 1939, when Noel Baddow 'Bill' Pope, riding a modified Brough with a JAP engine, clocked an astounding average of 200.38 km/h (124.51 mph) for a lap. No one had a chance to equal that record, as shortly afterwards war broke out and Brooklands closed its doors for ever. Bomb damage took its toll (the AVRO aircraft factory was within the grounds), and by the time the last all-clear sounded there was little chance that Brooklands would ever again echo to the sound of unsilenced racing engines.

Today all that's left is the old clubhouse and a short stretch of the legendary banking. In the postwar era, redundant wartime airfields were converted into racetracks and the character of closed-circuit racing changed to reflect improvements in the bikes' handling – negotiating a twisting course became more important than the pursuit of outright speed. It's a measure of that change that Thruxton is now the fastest closed circuit in the UK, with Niall MacKenzie and Yamaha holding the record at 'only' 174.34 km/h (108.33 mph).

But even on the few remaining ultra-fast road circuits it was an amazing 55 years before a lap record came anywhere near Pope's prewar feat.

In August 1994, the Ulster Grand Prix – a public-roads event with a history almost as long as the Isle of Man TT – saw an epic three-way battle in the two-leg Superbike race. In the first, over eight laps of the 12 km (7.4 mile) Dundrod course near Belfast, TT legend Joey Dunlop wrestled the win from Phillip McCallen and Jason Griffiths in an average speed of 198.32 km/h (123.23 mph).

In the second race Dunlop lost out as McCallen and Griffiths relentlessly upped the pace through the country lanes of Dundrod. From the third lap they never dropped below an average 200 km/h (124 mph). Eventual winner McCallen described the race later as the toughest he'd ever had. Coming from a multiple TT winner, that's something, but it was 21-year-old Welshman Griffiths who had the last laugh – chasing McCallen, he'd set a fastest lap of 202.94 km/h (126.1 mph), a new British record, and finally enough to top Pope's Brooklands best.

Overleaf: Mike Grainger on his turbocharged ZZR100 Kawasaki (see page 121).

Left: Noel B. Pope on the Brough that set the first two-wheel speed record at Brooklands on the eve of the Second World War.

World's fastest road circuit
Barry Sheene at Spa-Francorchamps, Belgium, 1977

IT IS ONE OF THE IRONIES OF MODERN RACING THAT, AS MACHINERY RELENTLESSLY INCREASES IN POWER AND SPEED, FOR SAFETY REASONS THE CIRCUITS THEMSELVES BECOME SLOWER. Of those circuits hosting races for the very fastest racing machines – 500 cc two-stroke Grand Prix racers – few see average speeds of greater than 177 km/h (110 mph), with many under 160 km/h (100 mph). Only Germany's blisteringly fast Hockenheimring, where the lap record now approaches 209 km/h (130 mph), is the exception.

Not very long ago, it was different. Few Grand Prix circuits were purpose-built. Most, like the Isle of Man TT circuit, were normal country roads closed for the duration. Almost all these 'road circuits' were frighteningly, vividly quick. But the quickest of all was in the picturesque

and hilly Ardennes region of south-east Belgium: the legendary Spa-Francorchamps. As well as being the fastest this is the second oldest circuit in the world still in use, after the Isle of Man.

On 3 July 1977, Barry Sheene, riding a factory four-cylinder RG500 Suzuki, lapped the circuit at 217.37km/h (137.151 mph) on the way to winning the 500 cc Grand Prix. On the same glorious day the smaller classes showed equally stunning pace. Walter Villa recorded a lap at 208.74 km/h (129.71 mph), riding a 250 cc two-stroke Harley-Davidson; even the 50 cc Kreidler of Eugenio Lazzarini averaged 162.8 km/h (101.16 mph) for the entire race.

The 14.12 km (8.774 mile) Spa circuit formed a rough triangle between the town of Francorchamps and the villages of Malmédy and Stavelot (it did not actually touch the genteel town of Spa). Combining searingly fast corners and hairy plunges into villages and valleys, it was first used in 1921 and held its first world championship Grand Prix event in 1949. Britain's Bill Doran won on an AJS while Arciso Artesiani took the fastest lap on a Gilera at 154.94 km/h (96.28 mph).

Above and left: Barry Sheene taking the lead on his four-cylinder RG500 Suzuki in the 1977 Belgium Grand Prix.

From there, lap records rose relentlessly, until safety concerns caused the abandonment of the 'long' road circuit after 1978. Instead, a new 6.94 km (4.31 mile) short circuit was constructed, using several sections of the former track but omitting Malmédy and Stavelot and with an entirely new loop with slower bends and wider run-off than before. The new circuit is nonetheless open to normal road traffic on non-race days.

Inevitably lap speeds fell dramatically. When the new circuit was first used for a 500 cc Grand Prix on 1 July 1979, the lap record was over 72 km/h (45 mph) slower than before, and it was to be another four years before Kenny Roberts exceeded even 160 km/h (100 mph). Spa-Francorchamps has not been used for motorcycle Grands Prix since 1990, although it continues to host a world championship 24-hour endurance race each year, as well as the F1 car Grand Prix. The new Spa-Francorchamps may be much slower than the old, but it retains much of the classic circuit's former atmosphere and charm.

Fastest man on two wheels
David Campos at Bonneville Flats, 1990

THE TRADITION OF MOTORCYCLE SPEED ACHIEVEMENTS SPANS THE TWENTIETH CENTURY.

It was in 1920 at Daytona that Ernie Walker set a record of 167.56 km/h (104.12 mph) on an Indian 994 cc mount. This achievement was followed in 1930 by Joe Wright of the UK, a well-known racer at Brooklands, who reached 242.45 km/h (150.65 mph) on a 998 cc Zenith/JAP.

The Bonneville Salt Flats in Utah, used by so many record-breaking vehicles because of its exceptional flatness, drew international attention in the 1930s when Utah driver Ab Jenkins lured British racer Sir Malcolm Campbell to compete for speed records on the salt surface. By 1949, the raceway on the Bonneville Salt Flats was the standard course for world land speed records. On this natural straightway the 300, 400, 500 and 600 mph land speed barriers were broken.

In 1950, Roland E. Free set a world motorcycle speed record of 252.2 km/h (156.71 mph) and then in 1956 the German Wilhelm Herz raced his 499 cc NSU through the 322 km/h (200 mph) barrier to clinch 340.2 km/h (211.40 mph). A streamlined machine called 'the Brute', which attained a speed of 361.64 km/h (224.71 mph) in 1958, broke the record. In 1970, Cal Rayborn broke the record again with a streamliner at 427.26 km/h (265.49 mph).

In 1978 the American Don Vesco broke through 300 mph (482.80 km/h), riding a double-inline-engined (estimated 2030 cc) Kawasaki bike over the Bonneville Flats to clock up a stunning 512.734 km/h (318.598 mph).

The Bonneville Flats was also the venue chosen for the 1990 motorcycle speed attempt. Dave Campos rode a huge 7 m (23 ft)-long streamliner called 'Easyriders', which was powered by two Ruxton Harley-Davidson engines. His faster run was at an average speed of 519.609 km/h (322.87 mph), and he set AMA and FIM records with his overall average speed of 518.45 km/h (322.15 mph).

In 1997, further attempts were being made to break this record by a team financed by Max Lambky of Virginia, USA, who claimed to have put approximately $100,000 into the project. The two-wheeled vehicle was a 6 m (20ft)-long, cigar-shaped chassis on which were mounted two coupled Vincent 1000 cc engines with a claimed power output of 414 bhp (rpm not released). The rider was Stu Rogers of Wisbech, England, who has won several times on Classic Nortons in the Classic class races during Daytona Speed Week.

The tradition lives on, as veteran Don Vesco was proving at Bonneville in 1997, when he gave his support to the latest record-breaking attempt by conducting his own tests of the new two-wheeler, believed to be capable of exceeding 563 km/h (350 mph). Until the true capability of this machine is proven under the strict regulations of the governing bodies for motorcycle speed records, the achievement of Dave Campos – the fastest man on two wheels – will stand.

Opposite: Carl Fogarty
recording the fastest lap at
the Isle of Man TT.

Narrowing the gap
Fogarty's fastest lap at the Isle of Man TT Races, 1992

CARL FOGARTY'S SENSATIONAL SIXTH AND FINAL LAP DURING THE TT RACE ON 12 JUNE 1992 WAS THE FASTEST EVER RECORDED at the world-famous motorcycle race event contested annually over public roads on the Isle of Man. And yet, despite completing the circuit in 18 min 18.8 sec at a speed of 198.93 km/h (123.61 mph), he was beaten to the finishing line!

Renowned for its tortuous twists and turns, the Isle of Man course has posed stiff challenges to motorcyclists since the first race took place over the St John's Short Course on 28 May 1907. On this historic occasion, Charlie Collier rode a Matchless machine at 61.51 km/h (38.22 mph) to become the first winner of the Marquis de Mouzilly St Mars Trophy in the single-cylinder class, while Rem Fowler took the Dr Hele-Shaw Trophy for his win on a Norton at 58.29 km/h (36.22 mph) in the multi-cylinder race. Each man picked up £25 in prize money. Since it was adopted in 1911, the longer Mountain Course has posed ever-greater challenges to riders, not least the difficulty of remembering and mastering every dip, undulation and bend of rural public road over a six-lap race of 364.4 km (226.4 miles).

It was expected that the 1992 event was going to be fiercely contested – but nobody was to know that this was to be one of the closest neck-and-neck races in TT history. Riding a 750 cc Yamaha bike, Carl Fogarty led the first lap by 1.2 sec. At the grandstand on the second lap, it was Fogarty's rival Steve Hislop who took the lead by 3 sec despite having to have the rear wheel on his twin-rotary-engined 588 cc Norton changed at the pit stop. At the third, the roles were reversed as Fogarty surged ahead of Hislop once more by 3.8 sec. As they completed the fourth lap, Hislop notched up a lead of 8.4 sec over Fogarty even though he had had another slow pit stop caused by a troublesome fuel cap. At the fifth, Hislop clung on tenaciously to his lead, although Fogarty narrowed it slightly to 6.4 sec. Fogarty and Hislop were achieving such speeds over the treacherous circuit that both men and machines were seen to take off each time they hit the notorious hump on the straight known as Cronk-y-Voddy at over 225 km/h (140 mph).

By the sixth, both riders benefited from the lighter weight of their bikes because their tanks were emptier and the

Despite walking away without the trophy at the Isle of Man TT race in 1992, Carl Fogarty still managed to record the fastest lap ever.

machines consequently over 23 kg (50 lb) lighter, having used 27–36 litres (6–8 gal) of fuel since filling up at the fourth. As they entered the sixth lap, the race had all the makings of a classic duel between two of the sport's most determined and experienced riders. Steve Hislop was not about to give up his hard-earned lead and he blasted round the course to victory. Hot on his heels was Carl Fogarty, who shaved his rival's lead to a mere 4.4 sec, storming to a lap record that still stands. The motorcycle press declared the race to be the most exciting TT since the legendary Hailwood and Agostini battle in 1967.

Street-legal and raring to go
The highest motorcycle speed in the UK, 1996

THE MOST ASTONISHING ASPECT OF THE BRITISH MOTORCYCLE SPEED RECORD IS NOT SO MUCH THE SHEER SPEED INVOLVED, AS THE FACT THAT IT IS HELD BY A STREET-LEGAL ROAD BIKE. At Elvington Airfield, York, on 21 March 1996, Plymouth motorcycle dealer Mike Grainger put his turbocharged ZZ-R1100 Kawasaki through the timing lights at a speed of 336.44 km/h (209.05 mph). This is also a European speed record.

The previous record, set by a purpose-built rotary-engined Norton streamliner, was set at 322 km/h (200.08 mph) in 1991. Grainger's achievement was all the more remarkable on several other counts. It was windy and bitterly cold that day, and a faulty ignition box prevented the Kawasaki from reaching its true potential. And, with only a 1.2 km (³/₄ mile) run-up to the measured quarter mile (0.4 km), Elvington is not really long enough for any machine to achieve its true maximum speed. In effect, it had to accelerate from rest to over 338 km/h (210 mph) in around 1190 m (1300 yards).

In order to qualify as an official record, a machine must achieve two runs in opposite directions, the mean average of the two being the recognized speed. Grainger's two runs were timed at 330.67 km/h (205.47 mph) and 342.40 km/h (212.76 mph) respectively, some way below the 357 km/h (222 mph) he achieved on the same machine a year earlier during a one-way run at Bruntingthorpe, Leicestershire. Should Grainger need to raise his game, the potential is there.

Reaching such speeds requires prodigious horsepower. The 16-valve four-cylinder Kawasaki is overbored to 1108 cc and runs a Garret T25 turbocharger running at 21 psi. A simple but effective fuel injection system replaces the Kawasaki's carburettors. Power output is comfortably in excess of 300 bhp.

To help the engine cope with the enormous stresses involved, it uses 116 octane fuel, plus 50:50 water/methanol injection to cool the piston crowns. Brian Capper painstakingly built the engine, with lots of special metal treatments, special pistons and con-rods, and improved oiling. Since 300 horsepower tears the standard Kawasaki transmission to pieces, a special 'Orient Express' centrifugal lock-up clutch, like that commonly used on drag bikes, was also preferred.

The power this device produces is simply awesome. Crack open the throttle in top gear at 240 km/h (150 mph) and, despite a lengthened swing-arm, the front wheels paw the air. A standard ZZ-R1100, capable of over 274 km/h (170 mph), feels utterly flat in comparison. 'I use it quite a lot on the road,' admits Grainger, as though discussing commuting, his soft Devon burr disguising the terminal speed psychosis beneath. 'When I need a fix, I take it for a spin.' So, a word of advice: if you should see a blue, white and yellow ZZ-R next time you're in Devon, don't be tempted to play. It could well be the British and European speed record-holder.

Since Grainger hurtled his Kawasaki through the Elvington timing lights, at least two rocket-powered motorcycles have made attempts on his record. Both have failed. On the short record strips available in Europe, 322 km/h (200 mph)-plus is no easy matter.

Left: *Mike Grainger, the motorcycle dealer from Plymouth who holds the British motorcycle speed record.*

Right: *Grainger on the street-legal turbocharged ZZR100 Kawasaki that broke the British record in 1996.*

Honda
From a tiny shack to world number one

THE WORLD'S LARGEST AND MOST POWERFUL MOTORCYCLE MANUFACTURER CAME FROM HUMBLE BEGINNINGS. Unique among the Japanese factories, Honda had no existing manufacturing base when founder Soichiro Honda, a 40-year-old engineer, bought up 500 war-surplus two-stroke engines and fitted them to bicycles, making a crude but effective moped. That was in 1946. The following year he was making his own engines; in 1948 the Honda company was officially formed and by 1949 complete machines were rolling out of Honda's 'factory' – a tiny shack on a bombsite.

The first four-stroke was made in 1951, but the real breakthrough came in 1958 with the Super Cub, a 50 cc, step-thru scooter designed to appeal to the commuter. It was reliable, cheap to run and easy to maintain. Demand was staggering – enough to propel Honda from minor maker to world number one in a couple of years. Forty years on, versions of the Cub are still being made all over the world, and production has topped the 20 million mark. It's the solid basis on which so much of Honda's later success rests.

But that wasn't enough for Honda, and in 1959 he went racing, turning up at the Isle of Man TT to hoots of laughter from the British. The following year Hondas came fourth, fifth and sixth in the 250 cc race. In 1961 they took racing into a new era with a massive team effort that brought them the top five places in both TT races and a staggering 18 Grand Prix wins out of 22. No one was laughing any more.

The Sixties brought the CB450 – the legendary Black Bomber – but it was the CB750 of 1969 that really set the world on fire. It was the first mass-produced four-cylinder machine, and featured disc brakes and electric starting. It was the bike that killed off the British motorcycle industry and was the pattern for sports-bike design for over 15 years.

Honda's strength is that it has always fired the imagination with the most technologically advanced bikes in the world, but has never lost sight of the fact that most people need something more practical. Since 1988, while first the ground-breaking V4, RC30 superbike,

then the revolutionary, oval-pistoned, £37,000 NR750, and later the £18,000 RC45 have all kept Honda at the cutting edge, the gradually evolving CBR600, with its relatively mundane specification, has proved the best seller among road riders year after year.

On the racetrack, Honda goes into its 40th birthday year with the number-one plates in 500 cc and 250 cc Grands Prix, courtesy of Mick Doohan and Max Biaggi, and World Superbikes with John Kocinski. Doohan has won the Blue Riband class an amazing four years in a row, underlining Honda's technical dominance.

Soichiro Honda died in 1992, but his ethos of continuous innovation lives on. The year he died, the 900 cc Fireblade took supersports machines to new levels of performance and handling – six years on, Honda's rivals are only just beginning to catch up.

Left: *Honda have been market leaders in motorcycle design and production since the company was formed in 1949, continually producing faster, sleeker and more innovative models.*

Opposite: *the Honda VF 1000R, launched in 1985, followed Honda's pattern of producing both great racing bikes and more practical machines.*

Kawasaki
Planes and boats and trains – and motorcycles

ALTHOUGH KAWASAKI IS THE SMALLEST AND YOUNGEST OF THE JAPANESE MANUFACTURERS, ITS PARENT COMPANY, KAWASAKI HEAVY INDUSTRIES, IS ONE OF JAPAN'S BIGGEST AND OLDEST. Motorcycles are just a small part of an operation that includes shipbuilding, trains, aircraft and steelworks.

It was the aircraft company's need to diversify after the war that led directly to Kawasaki's involvement in motorcycles. In the Fifties it supplied engines to other manufacturers, and when Kawasaki wanted to move into full-scale production, it took the sensible step of buying up one of those makers, Meguro, rather than starting from scratch.

Opposite: the power behind the 1979 Kawasaki Z1300.

Below: the 1980 shaft drive Kawasaki 1000 – today the company are still producing mould-breaking street bikes.

The first bike to carry the Kawasaki name was a 125 cc two-stroke, the B8 of 1962, but most of the early bikes were based on British twin-cylinder machines of up to 650 cc, and some were almost direct copies.

Deliberately aiming at the performance market, from 1969 Kawasaki produced a range of large, three-cylinder two-strokes that had a reputation for wild handling and huge power, but four-stroke development continued.

In late 1968, Kawasaki was nearly ready to deliver its shock blow to the motorcycling world – a 750cc, overhead-cam superbike that would revolutionize the market. But at the Tokyo show of that year, Honda unveiled their frighteningly similar CB750 and got it on sale first. Kawasaki went back to the drawing-board, updated and refined the design and finally launched the Z1 for the 1973 model year. The main crucial change was a leap in capacity from 750 cc to 903 cc, and the Z1 beat the Honda hands down. It went on to become the sports-bike of the Seventies and, perhaps as importantly, to mark out the 900 cc format as being Kawasaki's own territory.

In racing, Kawasaki has had a chequered history, partly because of its avowed policy of modifying road bikes for racing rather than building pure race bikes. It won its first world title, in the 125 cc class, in 1969 (British rider Dave Simmons's victory was largely due to Yamaha's and Suzuki's withdrawal from GPs that year), but Grand Prix success in the larger classes was elusive until Mick Grant took Kawasaki's first 250 cc win in 1977. That was followed by four years of Kawasaki domination in 250s, courtesy of Kork Ballington and Anton Mang, who took two titles each between 1978 and 1981. But Kawasaki never won the 500 cc title and eventually withdrew from GPs to concentrate on World Superbike, where Scott Russell was champion in 1993, and Endurance, where Kawasaki has always been strong.

It is four-strokes that are Kawasaki's main business. In 1984 it reproduced its mould-breaking feat with the GPZ900R, a fast, fine-handling sports-bike that was so well engineered that the engine was used as the basis for Triumph's 'new' design six years later.

In 1998 the company is still producing 900 cc street-bikes with excellent performance and handling – the latest Ninja ZX-9R is one of the most versatile and sought-after supersport bikes of the year.

Suzuki

From rags to riches on the superbike trail

WHEN SUZUKI WON THE 50 CC WORLD TITLE IN 1962, JUST 10 YEARS AFTER SWITCHING FROM TEXTILES TO MOTORCYCLES, it was the start of a long and distinguished racing record. Suzukis went on to dominate the 50 cc class for the next six years, and to make their mark in the other classes too. In fact, the only class Suzuki have never won is the 250 cc – ironically, since Suzuki's road range has always included some of the best 250 cc race replicas.

But the real glory days for Suzuki were in 500s. Barry Sheene's two titles in 1976 and 1977 should have been joined by a third – he was robbed by a breakdown in the last race. In 1981 Marco 'Lucky' Lucchinelli brought it back to Suzuki, and the next year Franco Uncini kept it there.

In the early Nineties fans thrilled to the epic battles between Yamaha-mounted Wayne Rainey and Suzuki's Kevin Schwantz. Schwantz put his heart and soul into racing – often riding injured and always at 110 per cent; he won races but crashed a lot and always seemed to miss the title until finally making it in 1993.

With its emphasis on racing success, Suzuki stuck to what it knew best – small to mid-weight two-strokes – all the way through the Fifties and Sixties. But when it decided to branch out, it did it big time. While other manufacturers followed Honda's lead to produce large, complex four-strokes, Suzuki launched two alternative superbikes in 1971 – the three-cylinder, water-cooled, 750 cc, two-stroke GT750, and the radical Wankel rotary-engined RE5. Although technically advanced, smooth and powerful, the RE5 didn't click with the public and was soon dropped, but the GT750 was an instant classic.

Suzuki had bided its time before going into the four-stroke market, learning from Honda's CB and Kawasaki's Z1, and finally launching the GS750 in 1976. It was fast, good-looking and a huge success, and so well-engineered it was later built in 1000 cc and 1100 cc versions; it is still popular with drag racers today. The GT750 was still available, and Suzuki was the only maker to offer superbike buyers a choice of two- or four-stroke machines – a trend continued in the Eighties when the 500 cc two-stroke RG500 gave road riders a taste of the Grand Prix experience.

But the real breakthrough, the bike that made Suzuki's modern reputation, was the GSX-R750 in 1985. At a time when 'superbike' meant 1100 cc, steel frame, 209 km/h (130 mph) and 250 kg (550 lb), the GSX-R offered just 750 cc, but with its alloy frame (the first on a production bike) weighed just 176 kg (388 lb), and blasted to 240 km/h (150 mph). More importantly, it handled like no other road bike. For years the GSX-R was the privateer racer's choice, as well as the road-going hooligan's preferred mount. Thirteen years and eight updates later, the current GSX-R is 32 km/h (20 mph) faster, and boasts fuel injection and computer-controlled engine management. But the basic ethos remains the same – it's one of the maddest road bikes you can buy.

The Suzuki GT750 – the first breakthrough bike for Suzuki – was an instant success with the public and remains a favourite for drag-racing today.

Yamaha
Music to your ears

T FIRST GLANCE THERE'S NOT MUCH CONNECTION BETWEEN PIANOS AND MOTORCYCLES, but like most Japanese manufacturers Yamaha came to motorcycling after huge success in other fields – in this case as a maker of high-quality musical instruments. But between pianos and motorcycles came the war, and Yamaha's factories were switched to aircraft production. In peacetime, a switch to two wheels was equally natural.

The first Yamaha bike – a two-stroke single based on the German DKW – came along in 1954. In 1957 came the 250 cc two-stroke twin, starting a trend that lasted 30 years.

Yamaha stuck with two-strokes until 1969, when the XS1 was launched. It was a 650 cc twin derived from British designs of the Sixties and was blown out of the water by Honda's radical CB750 of the same year.

The Seventies brought the three-cylinder XS750 and a range of four-cylinder bikes – big, heavy machines with a big, heavy image. It wasn't until 1985 and the FZ750 that Yamaha's four-stroke image changed. That was the start of a phenomenally successful range of four-strokes from the OW01 race bike to the brand-new YZF1000R1 – 1998's top sports-bike.

But the basis of Yamaha's reputation was always the race results of its two-strokes – underlined when its road-going twins were given the Race Developed tag – RD for short. In the early Sixties, much of the development had actually been done by MZ's brilliant designer, Walter Kaaden. MZ's works rider, Ernst Degner, defected from East Germany in 1961 and took a lot of Kaaden's secrets with him to Japan. The head-start he gave to Yamaha's race bikes filtered through to the road bikes and gave them an edge the competition struggled to match.

Yamaha won its first Grand Prix in 1963, taking the title the following year with Phil Read on a 250. But the Blue Riband class had to wait until 1975, when Giacomo Agostini took a Yamaha to the 500 cc title, breaking MV Augusta's 17-year stranglehold. Since then, Americans Kenny Roberts, Eddie Lawson and Wayne Rainey have taken three titles each to make it 10 for Yamaha – more than any other manufacturer except MV.

But over the same period the two-stroke road market was slowly dying. Its heyday was the early Eighties – the seminal RD250 and 400 of the Seventies gave way to the RD250LC (for Liquid Cooled). As essential to the two-wheeled hooligan as the Ford Capri was to his four-wheeled counterpart, it became the bike for ↘ production racing, and is still a cult bike today. A 350 cc version followed, then the YPVS, an updated version with a Powervalve – Yamaha's innovative exhaust system, which combined peak power with mid-range driveability.

The last-gasp effort to revive the glory days was the TZR250 in 1987, last in that great line of parallel twin-strokers and all-conquering in its class until the Suzuki RGV250 stole its thunder in 1990. These days Yamaha's future is with four-strokes, and with the YZF1000R1, the future looks bright.

Above: the Japanese have dominated the motorcycle market for many years and Yamaha have been manufacturing two-wheelers since 1954.

Overleaf: the 1979 Yamaha 750 shaft drive, just one in a long line of immensely popular motorcycles. Today, the company concentrate on their four-strokes.

Speed + power = superbike
Top 10 most powerful production bikes

SOME PEOPLE ALWAYS DEMAND THE ULTIMATE IN SPEED and power. These 10 bikes represent the fastest, best-handling bikes in the world – the nearest the manufacturers will let us have to racing performance on the road.

Honda CBR900RR Fireblade (Japan)

Engine size	918 cc
Weight	183 kg (403 lb)
Power	126 bhp at 10,500 rpm
Top speed	269 km/h (167 mph)
Standing	0.4 km (1/4 mile) in 10.8 s at 212 km/h (132 mph)
Introduced	1997

Since the first Fireblade was launched in 1992, it has been the bike all the other manufacturers dearly want to beat on performance and sales figures alike. It is not the most powerful or the fastest bike, but it is so useable and handles so well on the road that minor updates have kept it out in front so far.

Kawasaki ZZ-R1100 (Japan)

Engine size	1052 cc
Weight	233 kg (514 lb)
Power	134 bhp at 10,250 rpm
Top speed	280 km/h (174 mph)
Standing	0.4 km (1/4 mile) in 10.9 s at 220 km/h (137 mph)
Introduced	1993

For years the ZZ-R was the unchallenged king of high speed. Massive acceleration allied to a comfortable ride and unrivalled reliablity made the ZZ-R the choice for the long-distance mile-muncher in a hurry. And although Honda's Blackbird has taken the top speed tag, the ZZ-R is still awesome.

Bimota SB6R (Italy)

Engine size	1074 cc
Weight	190 kg (419 lb)
Power	156 bhp at 10,000 rpm
Top speed	282 km/h (175 mph)
Standing	0.4 km (1/4 mile) in 10.2 s at 212 km/h (132 mph)
Introduced	1996

Bimota has made a career out of taking Japanese engines from bikes that did not handle very well, clothing them in sexy Italian bodywork and making them very fast indeed. The SB6R takes the Suzuki GSX-R1100 engine and gives it a lighter, better-handling chassis and adds a few km/h top speed.

Yamaha YZF1000R1 (Japan)

Engine size	998 cc
Weight	177 kg (390 lb)
Power	150 bhp at 10,000 rpm
Top speed	not yet available
Standing	not yet available
Introduced	1998

Six years on from Honda's Fireblade, Yamaha strikes back with the R1. It's smaller, lighter, much more powerful and insanely fast. Whether that will make it a better road bike over time remains to be seen, but big numbers sell, and the YZF1000R1 is selling as fast as dealers can get them.

Suzuki TL1000R (Japan)

Engine size	996 cc
Weight	197 kg (434 lb)
Power	135 bhp, rpm not available
Top speed	not yet available
Standing	not yet available
Introduced	1998

In an attempt to break Ducati's hold on World Superbikes, Suzuki has produced a V-twin blaster that is more powerful and refined, but lacks the character of the Italian bike. The hugely torquey twin makes the Suzuki a devastatingly effective road bike and should help it do well on the track, too.

Suzuki GSX-R750 (Japan)

Engine	749 cc
Weight	179 kg (395 lb)
Power	126 bhp at 12,000 rpm
Top speed	269 km/h (167 mph)
Standing	0.4 km ($^1/_4$ mile) in 10.8 s at 209 km/h (130 mph)
Introduced	1996

Honda CBR1100XX Blackbird (Japan)

Engine size	1137cc
Weight	223 kg (492 lb)
Power	164 bhp at 10,000 rpm
Top speed	285 km/h (177 mph)
Standing	0.4 km ($^1/_4$ mile) in 10.6 s at 216 km/h (134 mph)
Introduced	1997

Touted by Honda as the first 296 km/h (180 mph) production bike, the Blackbird does not quite live up to the tag, but it is close. Given a howling tailwind it might make it, but what is more important is that the quest for speed has also produced a very useable day-to-day road bike – go for top speed or go to the shops, whichever you like.

Successor to the original race replica (the first GSX-R750 of 1985), the current bike is as close to a World Superbike racer as you can buy off the shelf. It is the lightest in its class, and among the hardest-accelerating – wheelies are a fact of life on the GSX-R, and for 1998 fuel injection gives even more power.

Triumph T595 Daytona (Britain)

Engine size	955cc
Weight	198 kg (437 lb)
Power	128 bhp at 10,200 rpm
Top speed	256 km/h (159 mph)
Standing	0.4 km (¼ mile) in 11.1 s at 203 km/h (126 mph)
Introduced	1997

After producing worthy touring machines for a few years, the reborn Triumph factory upped their image with their first sports-bike, based on a tuned, fuel-injected version of the famous three-cylinder engine. Beautifully balanced for road riding, it was priced to compete with Ducati for the prestige end of the market.

Yamaha V-MAX (Japan)

Engine size	1198 cc
Weight	262 kg (578 lb)
Power	138 bhp at 8500 rpm
Top speed	225 km/h (140 mph)
Standing	0.4 km (¼ mile) in 10.3 s at 185 km/h (115 mph)
Introduced	1984

It's not exceptionally fast, it has no fairing, it doesn't stop and it dislikes like corners, but for the sheer drag-strip thrill of winding on the throttle, feeling the rear wheel spin and then skidding and skating off towards the horizon in a blur of noise and smoke, there is nothing to beat a V-Max on a sunny day.

Ducati 916 SPS (Italy)

Engine size	996 cc
Weight	195 kg (430 lb)
Power	125 bhp at 9500 rpm
Top speed	267 km/h (166 mph)
Standing	0.4 km (¼ mile) in 11.0 s at 203 km/h (126 mph)
Introduced	1997

Based on the all-conquering 916, the SPS was designed for production racing, so it got a tuned, big-bore engine and uprated suspension and braking parts. But it is a superb road bike as well, and despite a near-£20,000 price tag, Ducati quickly sold out and had to build more.

NASCAR

7

Somebody gets in front of me, hell, they ain't gonna be there for long.

Dale Earnhardt, multiple NASCAR champion

NASCAR *heroes*
The greatest of the stock-car racers

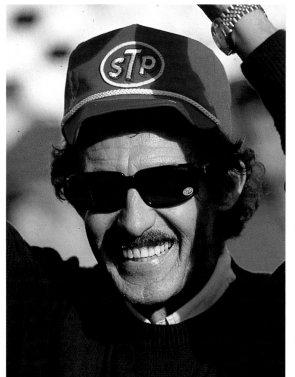

THE HISTORY OF STOCK-CAR RACING HAS BEEN DOMINATED BY A SERIES OF DRIVERS WHO RULED SUPREME IN THEIR ERA AND WERE DEIFIED BY THE HUGE NASCAR FOLLOWING. The greatest of them all was Richard Petty. Still regarded as the benchmark for all subsequent stock-car drivers, Petty's remarkable career rewrote the record books, setting standards that remain unbeaten to this day. This includes his incredible performance in 1967, when he steered his Plymouth to victory 27 times in 48 events.

He began his 34-year career in 1959, and the following season he won his first of a record seven NASCAR titles. He took 200 career wins from 1117 races, securing 127 pole positions along the way. Nicknamed 'The King', Petty also triumphed in stock-car racing's blue-riband event, the Daytona 500, seven times. Sponsored from 1972 by STP, he inspired the beginning of the corporate branding that adorns all stock-cars in the modern age. Petty caught the nation's imagination and helped steer the sport into the multi-billion-dollar show that is seen in homes across America, and beyond, today.

Petty achieved all his success in his home-run Petty Enterprises team, which was started by his illustrious father, Lee. Petty Senior was one of the first stars of stock-car racing, becoming champion three times in the 1950s, taking 54 victories and winning the inaugural Daytona 500 in 1959. The legacy of the racing Petty dynasty has been continued by Richard's son, Kyle. In 1992 'The King' finally retired as a driver but continues to run his team.

Richard Petty's domination of the sport was broken by several other great drivers, though. Most prominent among them was David Pearson, 'The Silver Fox'. A three-time champion, Pearson stands second only to Richard Petty in the all-time winners list with 105 career wins between 1960 and 1986, and it would have been more if he had not concentrated on racing only at the superspeedways, where he was more than capable of beating Petty.

Junior Johnson, known as 'The Lion Killer', attained mythical status in stock-racing circles as a driver and a team owner. He drove to 50 race wins, including the 1960 Daytona 500, before he retired. He then managed one of the most successful teams ever. He ran Cale Yarborough to an unprecedented hat-trick of titles between 1976 and 1978, and guided Darrell Waltrip to the Winston Cup crown three times in the early Eighties.

'You win some, lose some, wreck some,' Dale Earnhardt once said. This attitude epitomizes the aggressive nature of Earnhardt, 'The Intimidator'. He has dominated the modern era, and in 1994 scored a record-equalling seventh Winston Cup title. Many believe he is the only man on a par with Richard Petty and he has led the transition from Sunday racers to international superstars. But for the 46-year-old Earnhardt, time is running out to clinch that eighth title and, incredibly, a first victory in the Daytona 500.

Overleaf: Dale Earnhardt racing at the Atlanta Motor Speedway (see page 135).
Above: Richard Petty, the driver who has set the standard for all others.
Right: Earnhardt, nicknamed 'The Intimidator', the latest king of the stock-car circuit.

Atlanta Motor Speedway
The fastest of the NASCAR tracks

THE ATLANTA SPEEDWAY, GEORGIA, UNDERWENT A HUGE FACELIFT IN THE SUMMER OF 1997, with a lengthening of the superspeedway from 2.449 km (1.522 miles) to 2.48 km (1.54 miles) with a dog-leg on the pit straight. The back stretch became the front stretch, but the banked corners remained at 24°. The track was also resurfaced, which has allowed speeds to rise, making Atlanta currently the fastest track NASCAR visits.

Robby Gordon had previously held the highest speed of 300.154 km/h (186.507 mph) on the old layout. But qualifying speeds for the NAPA 500, on 15 November 1997, rose to more than 195 mph thanks to the supersmooth new surface.

Atlanta Speedway was built in 1960 and has been hosting NASCAR events since then. But since 1986, Atlanta's second race in November has been the last round of the Winston Cup. The NASCAR points system is such that more often than not the drivers' championship is still not decided when the circus arrives in Georgia. This has led to many thrilling finales, none more so than the Hooters 500 at Atlanta, which concluded the 1992 season.

Five drivers went to the race with a chance of securing the crown, including Alan Kulwicki, Bill Elliott and Davey Allison. At the beginning of the race Allison held fifth place, enough to take the title, until he crashed with Ernie Irvan and saw his hopes fade. By mid-distance, Elliott and Kulwicki had eased through the pack into a clear lead, and the cudgels started swinging. They lapped together flat-out for much of the race, but Kulwicki led most of the way and ensured himself the extra five points for leading the most laps. He was then able to pit and follow Elliott home in second place and lift the Winston Cup with a winning margin of just one point – the closest in the history of the sport.

That race was also the last for 'The King', Richard Petty, who retired. Unlike his glittering career, Petty's last race was an undistinguished one – he suffered an oil fire and retired. 'I went out in a blaze, but not much glory,' he said.

The Daytona and Talladega superspeedways were quicker than Atlanta, with Bill Elliott lapping both tracks at over 338 km/h (210 mph) in 1985. But stock-cars today have to run with restrictor plates at these two tracks, to keep speeds down. The restrictors are small pieces of metal placed over the air intake of the V8 engine's single-barrel carburettor, reducing the air flow and thereby cutting the power from 750 bhp to 400 bhp. The cars are still very quick but accelerate sluggishly, thereby reducing the overtaking opportunities.

This much-maligned safety procedure was introduced because the speedways simply could not get insurance cover when the cars were topping 320 km/h (200 mph). Thus, with speeds at Talladega and Daytona dropping to 298 km/h (185 mph), Atlanta is now the fastest track, and will remain so as long as the cars average less than that magic 320 km/h (200 mph) figure.

Dale Earnhardt racing at the Atlanta Motor Speedway, where recent modifications have transformed it into the fastest NASCAR track in the world.

Bristol Motor Speedway
Memories of the past

BRISTOL MOTOR SPEEDWAY, TENNESSEE, IS ONE OF ONLY THREE SHORT-TRACK OVALS REMAINING ON THE WINSTON CUP CALENDAR – unthinkable 40 years ago when they formed the basis of stock-car racing venues. The 0.857 km (0.533 mile) oval is longer only

The Bristol Motor Speedway in Tennessee is one of the last remaining short-track ovals used for stock-car racing.

than Martinsville, Virginia, and is one of the few remaining reminders of a bygone age.

Originally exactly 0.8 km (0.5 miles) long with 22° banking when it held its first premier stock-car race in 1961, Bristol was reconfigured in 1969 to measure 0.857 km (0.533 miles), with the steep 36° banking it sports today. The lap speeds at short tracks are much slower than on superspeedways, the fastest at Bristol being 201.317 km/h (125.093 mph), set by Mark Martin in qualifying for the Goody's 500 in 1995, but this still gives Bristol the tag of the 'World's Fastest Half Mile'.

With the growth of popularity of superspeedways, none of the ovals built over the last couple of decades has been a short track, and Bristol, Martinsville and Richmond are the only remaining short tracks in the

Winston Cup schedule – North Wilkesboro having been struck off the calendar in 1996. But the very reason for the growth of superspeedways itself holds the key to the bright future of Bristol. Superspeedways are preferred for economic reasons, not because of levels of the quality of racing. The seating capacity of a superspeedway is far higher than that of a short track, and with the huge stock-car following's hungry demand for tickets, this is the deciding factor. North Wilkesboro lost its race because it could hold only 40,000 spectators.

But Bristol is the exception to the rule, its huge, multi-tier grandstands being expanded again in 1998 to hold altogether 140,000 people, making it the fifth-largest stadium to host a stock-car race. And the tickets for the Bristol bi-annual races are sold out two years in advance. Bristol is also innovative and was the first track to introduce floodlights, to allow for night racing at its August race. In 1996, the circuit was bought by motor-sport mogul Bruton Smith, and its future now appears assured.

Although there are only a handful of short track races each year, the teams still build cars especially for the 0.8 km (half-mile) ovals, such is the difference in demands from a superspeedway. The cars feature a much bigger cooling system as there is less emphasis on aerodynamics. Much stronger brakes are used because of the tight turns, while the weight distribution and suspension geometry have to be altered.

The skills required to drive these cars on short tracks are also very different, and several drivers have excelled at them over the years. Darrell Waltrip, Winston Cup champion three times in the early Eighties, and a native of Tennessee, has won at Bristol 12 times, including a record-breaking seven times in a row, while Richard Petty was virtually unbeatable on short tracks, triumphing on them 145 times, a figure no one else has even approached.

Charlotte Motor Speedway
The 'Mecca of Motor Sports'

THE CHARLOTTE MOTOR SPEEDWAY IN NORTH CAROLINA IS ONE OF THE PILLARS ON WHICH THE WINSTON CUP HAS BEEN BUILT. Constructed in 1959 by current owner Bruton Smith, it was part of a wave of superspeedways, ovals of over 1.6 km (1 mile) in length, built in the late Fifties and early Sixties. Short tracks, usually about 0.8 km (0.5 miles) in length, such as Martinsville, had been running since the early Fifties, but there was a boom in superspeedways from 1959 to 1964 which revolutionised the sport, as high-banked, high-speed raceways attracted professional drivers and huge crowds, beginning the transition of the sport into the modern era.

Charlotte was built just after Darlington and Daytona, but before Talladega. These four tracks are considered today to be the 'crown jewels' of the Winston Cup. Charlotte is set deep in the heart of the South-West, where everyone lives and breathes sheet-metal V8 stock-cars, and from where many of the great NASCAR drivers originate. The Daytona 500 may be the most prestigious stock-car race, but the 600 lap race at Charlotte, sponsored by Coca-Cola since 1986, is the longest and is regarded as among the most arduous and physically demanding events.

No one has ever won all four 'crown jewel' races in one season, but LeeRoy Yarborough won three in 1969. The 'Silver Fox', David Pearson, matched that feat in 1976, including a win at Charlotte in the World 600, when he beat Richard Petty by seven seconds. That day is also remembered as the first time a woman competed in a Winston Cup race, when Janet

Guthrie finished 15th, while in 1988 Rusty Wallace won the first of his 47 career victories at Charlotte. In 1985, series sponsor Winston put up a $1 million prize for anyone who could match these hat-tricks, which Bill Elliott managed in 1985, and then Jeff Gordon repeated in 1997.

For founder Bruton Smith, Charlotte represented his dream superspeedway, and the 2.4 km (1.5 mile) oval hosted its first premier Grand National event on 19 June 1960.

The track features steeply banked corners at 24° connected by 5° straights, allowing speeds of up to 298 km/h (185 mph). Although the track struggled economically in its formative years, forcing Smith to sell up in 1962, he bought it Back in 1975 and has continued to enhance his facility so that Charlotte is not only one of the most historic tracks, but also one of the most developed. In 1992, Charlotte pioneered an overhead lighting system, using mirrors to avoid shadows encroaching on the track, which set up the excitement of night races for the Winston Cup at the 133,000-seater stadium.

That Hollywood chose Charlotte to shoot the film *Days of Thunder* starring Tom Cruise is testament to the fact that, for many, Charlotte remains the spiritual home of NASCAR racing and has earned its nickname as the 'Mecca of Motor Sports'.

Above and left: the Charlotte Motor Speedway, one of the cornerstones of stock-car racetracks, is considered the most difficult to master. Only the best go the distance here.

McLaren F1

Not so much a car as an expression of design philosophy

EGENDARY. THAT IS THE ONLY WAY TO DESCRIBE THE McLaren F1, a vehicle which was more an expression of design philosophy than a car. If you consider that the accelerator pedal alone is made up of six different titanium components, then you begin to understand the attention to detail that has been lavished on this extraordinary supercar.

Development started in 1990 when Gordon Murray (formerly of the Brabham Formula 1 team) delivered a concept briefing lasting 10 hours to a hand-picked team. This car was to be built without compromise, and the performance was to dictate the design, rather than vice-versa. Weight was a constant preoccupation for Murray; the initial target was set at 1000 kg (2204 lb), but the final all-up weight was 1140 kg (2513 lb) – still 40 per cent lighter than a Lamborghini Diablo. The reason why the mighty McLaren has only a weedy honk to warn of its imminent approach is that an air-horn was rejected as being too heavy. Similarly, Kenwood was approached to design a bespoke lightweight CD player (no radio, that is also too heavy). The majority of this weight – engine, transmission, occupants and fuel – was to be kept largely within the 2580 mm (101.57 in) wheelbase, in order to approach that holy grail of the vehicle designer's art: perfect weight distribution.

There is no turbo, ABS or traction control, all of which were deemed to pollute the purity of the driving experience. Besides, who needs traction control when you can pull from rest in any one of the specially developed six gears? It is gratifying to know that 96 km/h (60 mph) is yours in 3.2 s, 160 km/h (100 mph) is cracked in under 8, and that you can eventually power on to a maximum of 372 km/h (231 mph) (but what else would you expect from a car that delivers more torque – 69 kg/m (479 lb/ft) – than an F1 car)?

This grunt is achieved through a 48 valve, 6064 cc BMW engine, with VANOS variable valve timing. So what does all that mean? Other cars have a performance envelope. This has a performance regional sorting office. Quite simply, it's the fastest and most awe-inspiring car to drive, this side of ThrustSSC.

On the move, you have the benefit of active fan-assisted downforce, which constitutes almost a leitmotif of Murray's design ever since the Brabham-Alfa F1 fan car shot to fame, or notoriety, depending on your viewpoint.

The great paradox is that despite its £540,000 price tag the F1 is an incredibly simple, functional machine. It is a pure racer designed solely for aerodynamic proficiency. The fact that it is full of special touches, such as the gull-wing doors and the three-abreast seating layout, is incidental.

There are many who say that it has no place in modern society. They may be right: after all, no other manufacturer has attempted anything similar since. But as a testament to human achievement in engineering, it is immortal. Yes, even legendary.

Opposite: *the McLaren F1 exhibiting its sophisticated gull-wing design.*

Left: *the McLaren F1 – the fastest, smoothest, most awe-inspiring production car ever built? Probably.*

Mercedes-Benz

Where it all began

Above right: the 1926 Mercedes-Benz K.

Below: Karl-Friedrich Benz, founder of one of the greatest car manufacturers of the twentieth century.

FOURTEEN YEARS AGO MERCEDES-BENZ LAUNCHED THE 190 SERIES AS A COMPACT UPMARKET SALOON TO CHALLENGE THE BMW 3 SERIES. This was a drastic change in direction from a company renowned for building expensive executive barges. Now Mercedes-Benz has become even more radical with the launch of their revolutionary A-class, which is smaller than a Ford Fiesta but incorporates cutting-edge technology, while retaining the traditional Mercedes virtues of quality and luxury.

It was these 'traditional virtues' that had saddled Mercedes with a reputation for not being particularly innovative, ironically, given that the very first petrol-driven car in the world was the brainchild of no less than Karl-Friedrich Benz.

Born in 1844 in Karlsruhe, Germany, Karl-Friedrich was fascinated by mechanical transport. The wave of technology washing over the nineteenth century seemed not to have addressed the question of personal mobility: it was vaguely bizarre that Germany had built some of the largest factories in Europe yet people were still riding on horses as a means of transport. Karl-Friedrich set out to solve this problem and quickly established himself as an engine-builder, before venturing into the field of cars.

A small crowd was gathered on a cold morning in Mannheim in late 1885, to watch him unveil an odd-looking three-wheeled vehicle called a Motorwagen. Weighing in at approximately 250 kg (550 lb), his car was powered by a single-cylinder, four-stroke petrol engine capable of producing a heady 0.85 hp about 200 rpm. Maximum speed from the 577 cc vehicle was estimated at between 12 and 16 km/h (8–10 mph).

Its tubular steel chassis was incredibly simple, consisting of a U-shaped bend of metal, to which were bolted the various mechanical components and two spring-mounted seats with footboards.

Steering was – literally – a hit and miss affair, with a tiller connected to the solitary front wheel, thus eliminating the need to build a complex steering linkage. Suspension came from two double elliptic springs beneath the rear axle, as used extensively on stage coaches. The front wheel wasn't sprung at all and the solid rubber tyres would have contributed further to the eyeball-rattling ride.

Yet there were some remarkably advanced features as well, in particular the use of electronic ignition and mechanically operated inlet and exhaust valves.

Immediate contemporary reaction was mixed: the vehicle's first 1 km (0.6 mile) road test was reported in the local paper, the *Neue Badische Zeitung* under the heading 'miscellaneous'. The Motorwagen was patented on 1 January 1886 and, of the two original examples, one is still preserved in running order at the Daimler-Benz museum in Stuttgart.

That is the past, but what of the future? The trend seems to be towards downsizing and alternative fuel sources, but nobody really knows what the car of the future will be. We will just have to hope that an innovative and forward-thinking engineer like Karl-Friedrich Benz comes along with an answer.

Mercedes 300SL
Super Lightweight and very beautiful

THERE IS AN ARAB PROVERB THAT SAYS 'BEAUTY IS POWER'. THE MERCEDES 300SL IS FORTUNATE TO HAVE BOTH IN ABUNDANCE.

It is a visually stunning car which was not deliberately designed to be so. Following Mercedes's philosophy at the time of evolving road cars from its racing counterparts, the road-going 300SL was developed from the highly successful 1952 six-cylinder 300SL Sports Car, utilizing the distinctive gull-wing doors, which swing up instead of out and which contribute to the overall allure of the car. The 300SL was more about technology than style: it benefited from a revolutionary space-frame chassis and roof-mounted air brake.

The chassis took the form of two large cross-members joined by a lattice of smaller steel tubes. The tubes had to run beside the cockpit to give the car the necessary stiffness, hence the gull-wing doors. The lattice of tubes also meant that the dry-sumped engine had to be tilted at 50° in order to fit the bay. In 1952, its debut year of competition, this sports racer won Le Mans (with a factory one-two), the Carrera Panamericana and the Swiss and German Sports Car Grands Prix.

The thinking at Stuttgart was, however, that the car needed more power, and hence the 300SLR was born (the initials denoting Super Lightweight Racing car). This eight-cylinder monster pumped out 310 brake horsepower at 7500 rpm and was good for 260 km/h (160 mph).

It was this car that won the epic 1955 Mille Miglia race through Italy, piloted by Stirling Moss with the late Denis Jenkinson as navigator. Battered,

filthy, but still beautiful, Moss's car number 722 (which indicated the car's 7:22 a.m. start time) crossed the line ahead of the great Fangio's second-placed car, having averaged 157.65 km/h (97.94 mph) over 10 hours. The 300SLR went on to win the 1955 World Sports Car Championship.

The road car first appeared at the New York Motor Show in 1954 and soon became the choice of kings, dictators and Hollywood moguls alike. In 1957, an open-top roadster was introduced at the Geneva Motor Show, which strangely replaced the coupe rather than supplemented it. Of the two versions, the convertible is now the rarer, but the coupe is more valuable. A limited run of 29 all-aluminium gull-wing 300SLs was produced in 1954; one example was recently advertised for sale at $685,000!

The road-going 300SL's six-cylinder, three-litre engine produced 215 bhp at 5800 rpm, reaching a maximum speed a fraction shy of 260 km/h (161.55 mph). It was fitted also with Bosch fuel injection (incredibly advanced for the time) as opposed to the standard carburettors of the 300SLR. This helped it accelerate from 0 to 60 mph in just over eight seconds. Production of the roadster continued until 1963, by which time Mercedes had manufactured 1851 examples.

In its day, the 300SLR represented the apogee of automotive technological achievement, contained within a gorgeous, curvaceous, aerodynamic bodyshell. It will remain for many the ultimate 'Silver Arrow'.

Left: the 1956 Mercedes-Benz 300SL, the first car to employ the new space-frame chassis and roof-mounted air brake.

Right: the 300SL's distinctive gull-wing doors.

Porsche 917
The best racing car of all time?

THE PORSCHE 917 WAS VOTED THE BEST RACING CAR OF ALL time by a Motor Sport magazine jury in September 1997. The members of this jury, among others, were John Cooper, Paul Frère, Ron Dennis and Stirling Moss.

Still not convinced? Then read on. The sports-racing Porsche 917 debuted in 1969. Powered by a 4.9 litre normally aspirated flat 12 engine, it delivered 580 brake horsepower, revved to 8,200 rpm and exceeded 394 km/h (245 mph) on the straight – considerably faster than most of today's GT cars, which can expect to reach about 370 km/h (230 mph) flat out. It dominated its scene in a way that no other manufacturer could: Ferrari produced the (admittedly beautiful) 512S as a knee-jerk reaction to the Porsche's crushing dominance.

In the two seasons (1970 and 1971) that the Ferrari and the Porsche competed alongside each other, the Porsche won 14 times and the Ferrari just once. The 917 won the Le Mans 24 Hours twice, in 1970 and 1971, and took 15 world sports-car race wins between 1969 and 1971. Furthermore, it won two sports-car world titles (in 1970 and 1971), plus the World Can Am championship in 1973.

Such prodigiousness comes at a high price. The 917 was the enfant terrible of its day, demanding a degree of car control which was staggering. A savage, vicious beast is the only way to describe it.

Derek Bell, multiple winner of Le Mans, remembers vividly his first encounter with the beast, at a Hockenheim test session during the winter of 1970:

'Just before the stadium section I was running at about 170 mph in the dusk, when the headlight beam picked out a sight so unbelievable that for a split-second I thought I was hallucinating. There was a bloke cycling across the road, as cool as you like! ... at that speed I just dared not swerve a fraction, so I missed him by what seemed like the width of a cigarette paper. The look of sheer panic on his face is something that has stayed in my mind ever since.'

In 1971, Jo Siffert shared a special-version long-tailed Porsche 917 with Derek Bell for the latter's first Le Mans. Their car was clocked at 396 km/h (246 mph) – down the fabled Mulsanne Straight. Derek Bell has never been faster down there since. Unfortunately, his car dropped out with an oil leak, but the event was won by Helmut Marko and Gijs Van Lennep in a 917K entered by the Martini team.

The Porsche 917 is a beautiful dinosaur and it is certain that nothing like it will ever be seen again. The 917/30, the last of the evolutions, kicked out 1100 bhp in race trim, something that not even the fastest Formula 1 cars of the turbo and downforce era could ever hope to replicate. Its effect was stunning: in the 1973 American Can Am championship, the Porsche won every single race. And then, just as suddenly as it had come, it was gone. But never to be forgotten.

Opposite: the distinctive 1973 Porsche 917/30 Spyder.

Below: the Porsche 917, after winning the Le Mans 24 Hours in 1971 – the second time this model took the honours at this race.

The Supercars
12 of the world's fastest production cars

McLaren F1	372 km/h	231 mph
Jaguar XJ220	349 km/h	217 mph
Lamborghini Diablo	325 km/h	202 mph
Ferrari Testarossa	290 km/h	180 mph
Ferrari 348ts	277 km/h	172 mph
Ferrari 348tb	277 km/h	172 mph
Porsche 928 GT	274 km/h	170 mph
Porsche 911 Turbo	270 km/h	168 mph
Porsche 928S Series 4	266 km/h	165 mph
Porsche 911 Carrera 2	259 km/h	161 mph
Lotus Esprit Turbo SE	257 km/h	160 mph
TVR 450SEAC	257 km/h	160 mph

(The maximum speeds given are not necessarily officially confirmed.)

Above: *McLaren F1, the world's fastest production car.*

Left: *Jaguar XJ220, the highlight of the 1988 Motorshow.*

Below: *Lamborghini Diablo, speed and beauty combined.*

The Ferrari family—the Testarossa
(top left); the 348tb (bottom left);
and the 348ts (right).

*Porsche supercars: the 928 GT (**above***
***left**); the 911 Turbo (**below left**); the 928S*
*Series 4 (**above right**); the 911 Carrera 2*
*(**below right**).*

Right: the TVR450 SEAC.

Below: the Lotus Esprit Turbo SE. These share a top speed of 257 km/h (160 mph).

Trains and Railways

The resistance of the air which, in vulgar apprehension, passes for nothing, comes to be the greatest impediment to the motion of the vehicles, and may in some cases absorb five parts in six of the whole power.

Newspaper editor **Charles MacLaren,** on the motion of railway locomotives

Amtrak
219

The age of steam

Stockton and Darlington colliery line, 1825

RAILED TRUCKS HAD BEEN USED FOR MINING AS EARLY AS 1550 AT LEBERTHAL, ALSACE, AND BY RALPH ALLEN FROM COMBE DOWN TO THE RIVER AVON IN 1731, but the first self-propelled locomotive ever to run on rails was that built by Richard Trevithick (1771–1833) and was demonstrated over 14 km (9 miles) with a 10.2 tonne load and 70 passengers in Penydaren, Glamorgan, on 21 February 1804. The earliest established railway to have a steam-powered locomotive was the Middleton Colliery Railway. Set up by an Act of 1758 and running between Middleton Colliery and Leeds Bridge, Yorkshire, it was built by Matthew Murray in 1812.

Overleaf: LNER's high-speed breakthrough – The Silver Link (see page 167)

The Stockton and Darlington colliery line, County Durham, which ran from Shildon through Darlington to Stockton, opened on 27 September 1825. Here the 7.1 tonne Locomotion I (formerly Active) could pull 48.7 tonnes at a speed of 24 km/h (15 mph). It was designed and driven by George Stephenson (1781–1848). The first regular steam passenger run was inaugurated over a one-mile section (between Bogshole Farm and South Street) on the 10 km (6 mile) track between Canterbury and Whitstable, Kent, on 3 May 1830, hauled by the engine Invicta.

The very first electric railway was Werner von Siemens's 274 m (300 yd)-long Berlin electric tramway, opened for the Berlin Trades Exhibition on 31 May 1879. Several early train speed records were claimed by the US but were not authenticated and so the earliest rail speed record was claimed by the famous Stephenson's Rocket at the Rainhill Trials on the Liverpool and Manchester Railway on 8 October 1829, when it ran at 46.8 km/h (29.1 mph). This record was beaten on the opening day of the Liverpool and Manchester Railway on 15 September 1830, when Stephenson's 0-2-2 Northumbrian reached 58 km/h (36 mph) while conveying the fatally injured politician William Huskisson from Parkside to Eccles. This was then beaten on 13 November 1839 down Madely Bank in Staffordshire on the Grand Junction Railway by the 2-2-2 engine Lucifer.

The next three speed records were achieved on the Great Western Railway. In June 1845 the broad-gauge 2-2-2 Ixion reached a speed of 98.2 km/h (61 mph) between Didcot and London. On 1 June 1846 the 2-2-2 Great Western reached 119.5 km/h (74 mph) near Wootton Bassett, Wiltshire, and in the same place on 11 May 1848 the 4-2-2 Great Britain reached 125.5 km/h (78 mph).

The first speed record of the twentieth century was held by the aforementioned Siemens and Halske Electric railway near Berlin where a speed of 162.5 km/h (101 mph) was reached. This company managed to hold the speed record until 1904, reaching progressive speeds of 200.99 km/h (124.89 mph) on 6 October, 206.69 km/h (128.43 mph) on 23 October and 210.19 km/h (130.61 mph) on 27 October, all during 1903.

Left: LNER's Flying Scotsman hauled by Gresley Pacific Locomotive 4475, The Flying Fox.

Right: George Stephenson, who designed and drove one of the earliest steam-powered locomotives along the Stockton and Darlington line in 1825.

The Bullet Train
Courtesy of the Japanese Shinkansen, 1964

HE RAILWAYS OF JAPAN WERE PURCHASED BY THE GOVERNMENT ON 31 MARCH 1906 AND A RAILWAY BOARD WAS SET UP IN 1908. On 1 June 1949 the government railways were reorganized into a public corporation under the title of Japanese National Railways (JNR). From April 1987 JNR was split into seven separate railway companies of East Japan, West Japan, Hokkaido, Kyushu, Central Japan and Shikoku. Japan Freight Railway Co. operates nationwide freight services.

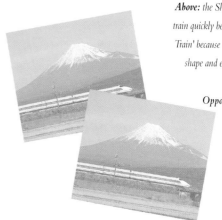

The Shinkansen Property Corporation leased the 1835 km (1140 miles) of standard-gauge passenger lines to the railway companies from 1987 to 1991; the network has now been sold to the three companies operating it. The title Japan Rail covers the whole organization. Of the 26,470 km (16,448 miles) that make up all Japan's railways, 16,040 km (9967 miles) are electrified. The Shinkansen (meaning 'new main line') system is electrified at 25 kV at both 50 and 60 Hz. In 1990–91 traffic on Japan Rail totalled 119,769 million passenger-km, with 5741 million passenger journeys.

It was Japan that first set the pace for modern, purpose-built, high-speed railways, and the inauguration of its services on the Tokaido Shinkansen line between Tokyo and Osaka in 1964 began the trend. With its sleek appearance and record-breaking speeds, the Shinkansen soon became known around the world as the 'Bullet Train'. The first regular scheduled service at over 161 km/h (100 mph) was introduced on this line on 1 November 1965, when trains began running the 516 km (321 miles) between Tokyo and Osaka in 3 hr 10 min at an average speed of 163 km/h (103.3 mph) with a maximum of 210 km/h (130 mph). These 12-car trains weighed 653 tonnes; they are nowadays 16 cars weighing 862 tonnes.

The line was extended to Hakata and the first trip from Tokyo to Hakata on 10 March 1975 covered the 1069.1 km (664.3 miles) in 6 hr 56 min at an average speed of 154.2 km/h (95.8 mph). During trials with a Series 961 train set in 1979 on the Shinkansen test track in Oyama, a speed of 319 km/h (198 mph) was reached. On 23 January 1980 JNR announced that trains on the Tohoku and Joetsu Shinkansen lines would operate at a maximum speed of 260 km/h (162 mph). In October 1985 the Class 925 reached a speed of 272 km/h (169 mph) on a scheduled test which was not beaten until 1990 by the 200 series on the Joetsu line, where a 275 km/h (171 mph) speed was reached.

Over the last years of the twentieth century the Shinkansen has gone from strength to strength, topping speeds as it goes along. By March 1997 the 500 series had entered limited service on the Sanyo Shinkansen, operating at a maximum speed of 300 km/h (186 mph), and JNR became the world's fastest train service.

Above: the Shinkansen Company's new train quickly became known as the 'Bullet Train' because of its gleaming streamlined shape and extraordinarily high speeds.

Opposite: established in 1970, the American company Amtrak has dramatically reduced travelling time and improved standards of service.

Amtrak, USA
Making trains worth travelling again, 1970

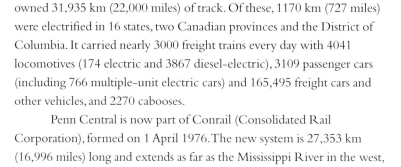

THE NATIONAL RAILROAD PASSENGER CORPORATION, KNOWN AS 'AMTRAK', WAS FORMED UNDER THE RAIL PASSENGER SERVICE ACT OF 31 OCTOBER 1970. It took over the passenger services of 22 leading US railroads. First operations began on 1 May 1971. The principal companies remaining outside the corporation were the Southern, Denver and Rio Grande Western, and the Rock Island and Pacific. The Amtrak operation now covers over 37,970 km (23,594 miles) connecting 440 cities in the US and into Canada, with 396 locomotives and 1929 passenger cars including sleepers, diners, dome cars and chair cars. Its aim is 'To make trains worth travelling again'. Amtrak has reduced the New York–Washington time to 2 hr 30 min for the 361 km (224 miles) with one stop, reaching an average speed of 144 km/h (89.5 mph), making it the world's fastest train service in 1970. It has now introduced the Swedish High Speed X-2000 which could reduce the journey by 15 minutes, travelling at 250 km/h (155mph).

The 'North Coast Hiawatha' is Amtrak's name for the former Northern Pacific 'North Coast Limited'. This streamlined train runs three times weekly, taking 50 hr 29 min over the 3586 km (2228 miles) between Chicago and Seattle. In the reverse direction, the time is 54 hr 25 min. These times give average speeds of 71 km/h (44 mph) and 66 km/h (41 mph).

In an attempt to achieve even greater efficiency, many of the railroad companies in the US combined into larger corporations. One of the first was the Penn Central, formed on 1 February 1968 by the merging of the Pennsylvania and New York Central railroads. On 31 December 1968 the New York,

Amtrak runs nearly 400 locomotives and 1929 passenger trains over thousands of miles across the US and into Canada.

New Haven and Hartford Railroad became part of the PC, which then owned 31,935 km (22,000 miles) of track. Of these, 1170 km (727 miles) were electrified in 16 states, two Canadian provinces and the District of Columbia. It carried nearly 3000 freight trains every day with 4041 locomotives (174 electric and 3867 diesel-electric), 3109 passenger cars (including 766 multiple-unit electric cars) and 165,495 freight cars and other vehicles, and 2270 cabooses.

Penn Central is now part of Conrail (Consolidated Rail Corporation), formed on 1 April 1976. The new system is 27,353 km (16,996 miles) long and extends as far as the Mississippi River in the west, Canada in the north, the Ohio River in the south and the Atlantic coast.

Railways carry 70 per cent of the coal in the US, 74 per cent of canned and frozen foods, 46 per cent of meat and dairy products, 71 per cent of household appliances, 76 per cent of cars and parts, 86 per cent of pulp and paper, 78 per cent of timber, 63 per cent of chemicals and 68 per cent of primary metal products. If the railways in the US were to shut down for one week then the national income for the year would be reduced by nearly 6 per cent. An eight-week shutdown would reduce the gross national product for the year by 24 per cent and increase unemployment by 22 per cent.

The IC
Making Italy's train service the world's fastest, 1988

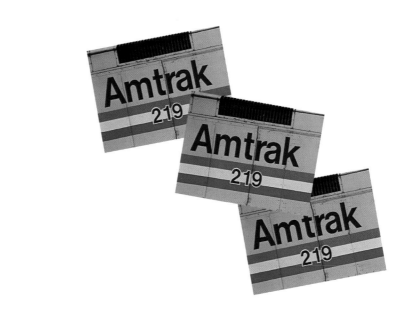

I N 1985 THE ITALIAN STATE RAILWAYS CHANGED ITS STATUS FROM A GOVERNMENT DEPARTMENT INTO A STATE CORPORATION. From 1992 the system was reconstituted as a state-owned commercial enterprise. It operates 16,066 km (9983 miles) of standard gauge of which 9799 km (6089 miles) are electrified at 3000V dc.

Because of the mountainous nature of the country many bridges and tunnels are needed. There are 43,158 bridges and viaducts with over 10 m (33 ft) length of clearance. Of these 39,091 are of masonry and 4067 of steel, of which 77 masonry and 31 steel bridges and 36 viaducts have a clearance over 100 m (328 ft) long. There are 1849 tunnels which total 911 km (566 miles). The longest is the Apennine, 18,519 m (11 miles 892 yd), and 21 others are over 5 km (3 miles) long. New lines are under construction with more large bridges and long tunnels soon to be completed.

By 1978 the famous Settebello trains were running the 218 km (135 mile) distance between Milan and Bologna in 104 minutes southbound and 102 minutes northbound. The latter represented a start-to-stop average speed of 130 km/h (80 mph). The central section of 96 km (60 miles) between Bologna and Florence is the slowest part, taking about 62 minutes. This is due not so much to the severe gradient in approaching the Apennine Tunnel but to the numerous curves leading up to the piercing of the mountain range.

By the 1980s Italy's IC trains were brought in. These were designed to reach running speeds of up to 280 km/h (174 mph) but in service the speeds are severely lower than this, owing to the nature of the Italian terrain. Each set typically comprises two power cars weighing 78 tonnes each, having a continuous power rating of 4800 kW (6432 hp) operating on a power supply of 3 kV dc. It was with the ETR450 IC train that Italy maintained the world's fastest train service in 1988 with an average speed of 141.3 km/h (87.7 mph) in 1988, losing the record to France's TGV Atlantique in 1989 and Sweden's X-2000 in 1990 before regaining the title in 1991 with the ETR500 series and then in 1992 losing out again to the Spanish AVE 100 series, which reached an average schedule speed of 158.9 km/h (98.7 mph).

In 1992 the last 44km (27 mile) segment of the Rome–Florence direttissima line was completed, reducing the track distance between the two cities and allowing the journey time to be cut to only 1 hr 25 min at an average speed of 185 km/h (155 mph). There are plans to improve and extend existing links, including a new tunnel through the Brenner Pass linking with Austrian Railways, and a high-speed (TGV) line from Lyons to Turin in co-operation with French Railways (SNCF).

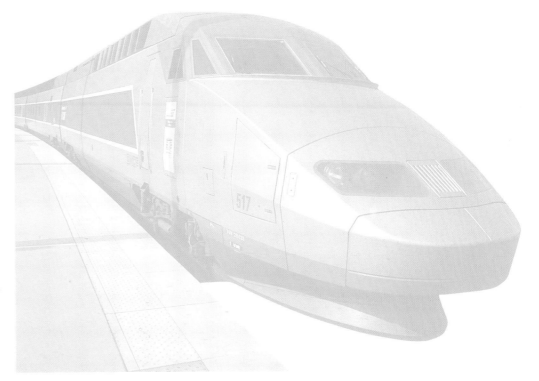

TGV Atlantique
Highest speed on a national rail system, 1990

RENCH NATIONAL RAILWAYS (SOCIÉTÉ NATIONALE DES CHEMINS DE FER FRANÇAIS; SNCF) WAS FORMED ON 31 AUGUST 1937 and took over the operating concessions of the major French railway companies on 1 January 1938. On 1 January 1983, the SNCF became a public corporation.

France has busily pursued a policy of building high-speed lines (Trains à Grande Vitesse; TGV). Trains on the TGV Sud Est line have been covering the 512 km (318 miles) distance from Paris to Lyons in two hours since 1983 while trains on the TGV Atlantique to Tours and Le Mans can run at up to 300 km/h (186 mph). The fastest point-to-point timing is one of 54 minutes for the 202 km (125 miles) from Paris to Le Mans, an average of 224 km/h (139 mph).

The new TGV Nord line to Lille and the Channel Tunnel opened in May 1993. Agreement was also reached in February 1993 to spend £2.5 billion on TGV Est, a 300 km (186 mile) stretch of line joining Paris and Strasbourg. Passenger traffic on French Railways rose from about £3000

French National Railways have concentrated on building high-speed lines across France, the fastest are these TGV trains, which have held the world speed record for ordinary rail vehicles.

million in 1987 to over £3800 million in 1991; total inter-city passenger travel grew from 48,800 million passenger-km in 1990 to 62,100 million passenger-km by 1995.

On the Sud Est line the TGVs are electric trains consisting of eight coaches and a power unit or locomotive at each end. The coaches are articulated on nine bogies to form one unit. The power units are on two four-wheeled power bogies, and another power bogie in the train makes a total of 12 motors normally working at 1070V 530 A. The motors are body-mounted to reduce unsprung weight. The trains have seats for 111 first-class and 275 second-class passengers. The nine-coach formations on the TGV Atlantique and TGV Nord lines run at up to 300 km/h (186 mph) but the Super TGV planned for the twenty-first century will seat up to 500 people in double-deck cars and run at speeds up to 350 km/h (217 mph).

The trains for the Channel Tunnel passenger service from Paris and Brussels to London are based on the successful TGV model. These TGV-Transmanche sets (Eurostar) operate at three different voltage settings for the three rail systems they have to run on – French Railways (25 kV 50 Hz), Belgian Railways (1500 V dc) and British Rail (750 V dc).

The TGV trains have held world speed records several times. On 26 February 1981 a TGV electric set No. 23016 attained a top speed of 380 km/h (236 mph) near Tonnerre in central France during a test run between St Florentin and Sathonay. The world speed record for ordinary rail vehicles on a public railway was achieved by a modified TGV Atlantique on 18 May 1990 when it reached a speed of 515.3 km/h (320.2 mph) near Vendôme on the line to Tours.

AVE
Spain takes over the mantle of worldbeater, 1992

SPANISH NATIONAL RAILWAYS (RED NACIONAL DE LOS FERROCARRILES ESPAÑOLES; RENFE) was formed under the law of 27 February 1943 when the government purchased the entire stock of the previous private railway companies and an autonomous corporation, nominally independent of the government, was set up to operate the railways. It operates 12,560 km (7805 miles) of 1676 mm (5 ft 6 in) gauge, of which 6419 km (3989 miles) are electrified at 1650 and 3000 V dc.

Since April 1992 trains have been running on the new Madrid–Seville high-speed line. This was built to standard 1435 mm (4 ft 8in) gauge (unlike the rest of the RENFE system, which at 1676 mm remains incompatible with the rest of Europe) and the AVE 300 km/h (186 mph) train sets cover the 471 km (293 miles) in a best time of 2 hours. The distance of the new line is 100 km (62 miles) shorter than the old route. This AVE track is similar to the one used with the ICE (Inter City Experimental), the German high-speed train. Between Madrid and Seville the switches are about 105 ft (132 m) in length and admit a top speed of 300 km/h (186 mph) and 160 km/h (99 mph) in derivation and eight engines are needed to activate them. In 1992 these AVE 100 series trains earned Spain the honour of becoming the world's fastest train service by running an average schedule speed of 156.9 km/h (97.5 mph) but the record was taken later that year by the Japanese Tokaido Shinkansen 300 series with an average speed of 206.2 km/h (128 mph).

AVE, which stands for Alta Velocidad Española (Spanish High Speed), is also being used for the Barcelona–Valencia line, where six broad-gauge AVE units reach a top speed of 220 km/h (137 mph). The AVE train sets are made in France with some Spanish components. They are directly derived from the French TGV Atlantique and are electrically powered by 25,000 V 50 Hz proportioned by a catenary system with concrete German masts. The train gets the electric power through two double pantographs installed in the rear part of the roof of each traction head. Eight cars are positioned between the two engines, which hold 313 seats in total, the complete length of the train being 200.114 m (656 ft 6 in). RENFE also use Talgo 200 trains, which cover the trajection Madrid–Huelva and Madrid–Cadiz using a variable gauge. The Talgo 200 train sets are pulled by electric locomotives class 252 which are fitted to run on AVE tracks with a top speed of 220 km/h (137 mph).

The costs of changing the gauge of Spanish rails or NAFA (as it is known) have overrun budget to the extent that the development of a Madrid–Barcelona–France high-speed standard-gauge line and gauge-conversion plans elsewhere in Spain have been delayed indefinitely.

Spanish AVE 100 series trains became part of the fastest service in the world, with an average scheduled speed of 156.9 km/h (97.5 mph).

Water Speed Records

10

Anything other than death is a minor injury.

Bill Muncey, multiple
Unlimited hydroplane
champion

Henry Segrave

King of speed on land and water, 1930

I N 1929, THE YEAR IN WHICH HE REGAINED THE LAND SPEED RECORD FROM AMERICA IN THE GOLDEN ARROW with a speed of 372.45 km/h (231.44 mph) on Daytona Beach, Major Henry Segrave also took a speedboat to America. Though better known as a Grand Prix driver and record-breaker on land, he had started racing boats in 1927 after American boat-racing legend Commodore Gar Wood gave him a couple of outings in his massive Miss America V. In 1928 Segrave approached Hubert Scott-Paine's British Powerboat Company to build him a new racer, which was designed by Fred Cooper. Miss England I used the same type of Napier Lion engine that had powered Golden Arrow, its 930 hp being transmitted to the water by a single propeller turning at the hitherto undreamed-of speed of 6500 rpm.

Segrave went from Daytona to Miami, where he began testing Miss England I in readiness for a duel with Wood. Wood's Miss America VII broke its steering quadrant in the first heat, which Segrave thus won. And though Wood won the second, Segrave had enough time in hand to take the overall victory in a much less powerful boat.

The next day Segrave averaged 147.91 km/h (91.91 mph) in six runs over a measured course, dramatically close to Wood's water speed record of 149.397 km/h (92.834 mph). Stung into defence, Wood himself edged his own record up to 149.86 km/h (93.12 mph), but the near miss set Segrave thinking.

While he continued to race Miss England I he was already planning a replacement. Miss England II was again designed by Cooper, who mounted twin Rolls-Royce R V12 engines in the stern, where they would drive the single propeller between 12,500 and 13,000 rpm. Critics immediately seized on this highly unorthodox concept as ammunition for attacking the design, and they also disliked the step upon which the front of the 11.5 m (38 ft) hull would run at very high speed. Segrave himself loved the craft, which was taken to Windermere in the Lake District in June 1930

for its first trials. There the speed king, now Sir Henry, experienced many of the frustrating mechanical problems that he had been fortunate to avoid during his land record exploits, as Miss England II consumed propellers. But by 13 June he was ready. The previous night he had declared, 'Either I shall break the record, or the propeller.'

With him travelled Vic Halliwell, a Rolls-Royce technician who used his holidays to help; and Michael Willcocks, a young mechanic. Segrave's first two runs yielded a new record at 158.93 km/h (98.76 mph), and then he prepared for an all-out run. They were travelling around 185 km/h (115 mph) when Miss England II struck something in the water and rolled over. Segrave succumbed shortly to his grievous injuries; Willcocks survived, and Halliwell's body was later recovered from the lake.

The English tragedy marked the first fatalities in the pursuit of speed on water, and in Segrave deprived England of motor sport's first true superstar.

Overleaf: Donald Campbell, continuing the work of his father Sir Malcolm, in the record-breaking Bluebird (see page 185).

Opposite: After breaking the world water speed record at Lake Windermere in 1930, Miss England II hit something under the water and overturned – Segrave and Halliwell were killed.

Above: the fearless Sir Henry Segrave, pilot of Miss England I and II, and the first man to perish in the pursuit of the water speed record.

Miss England II
Quickly flows the Don, 1931

FOLLOWING SEGRAVE'S DEATH ON WINDERMERE ON 13 JUNE 1930, MOMENTS AFTER HE HAD BROKEN THE WATER SPEED RECORD at a speed of 158.93 km/h (98.76 mph), Miss England II was raised from the lake and sponsor Sir Charles Cheers Wakefield, the founder of Castrol, decided to continue Segrave's work.

Damage to the craft was surprisingly light and it was rebuilt for the 1931 season. Wakefield hired another British racing driver, Kaye Don, to take over, and the plucky Michael Willcocks enrolled once again for the task of engineer, despite his tragic experience with Segrave. They were joined by Rolls-Royce technician Dick Garner.

Don had raced boats for some years, and had also been the driver of Sunbeam's unsuccessful Silver Bullet record car. Now he took easily to piloting Miss England II after the craft had been shipped out to the Parana River near Buenos Aires. By this time Gar Wood had regained his record with 164.40 km/h (102.155 mph), but after overcoming problems with the state of the Parana River and overheating engines, Don bravely ignored poor water conditions and on 2 April 1931 took the record back with 166.55 km/h (103.49 mph).

Don's next stop was Lake Garda in Italy, where Miss England II broke down in the Garda Shield race for the d'Annunzio Cup, but after further delays because of mechanical problems he broke his own record with an easy 177.381 km/h (110.223 mph). This time his mechanics were Garner and Roy Platford.

Miss England II was then shipped to Detroit for the prestigious Harmsworth Trophy race, but after Don won the first heat Gar Wood and his brother George became embroiled in controversy. Gar had deliberately jumped the start, duping Don into doing the same thing. Both were disqualified but, worse still, Miss England II capsized in Wood's wake. George Wood went on to win, and Gar Wood was branded as unsportsmanlike for his Yankee trick.

With the old boat now badly damaged, Wakefield commissioned Miss England III, which would use the same Rolls-Royce R engines but was much less unorthodox in design than her predecessor. Don went back to Lake Garda, but nose-heaviness prevented him from challenging Wood's record.

He then tried again on Scotland's Loch Lomond, but still mechanical problems troubled the attempt. Modifications were carried out, and on 18 July 1932 Don succeeded in raising the record to 188.98 km/h (117.43 mph). Dissatisfied, he tried again just before lunch, and became the first to travel at two miles a minute on water as he achieved another new record of 192.81 km/h (119.81 mph), with a best one-way figure of 193.92 km/h (120.50 mph).

Gar Wood, as indefatigable as Malcolm Campbell, had the last say in the battle with Wood, when Miss America X upped the record to 201.02 km/h (124.91 mph) on the St Clair River on 20 September that year. The great Anglo-American contest was finally over.

Right: British racing driver Kaye Don decided to continue Segrave's work and, after persistant mechanical problems with the rescued Miss England II, he built Miss England III.

Opposite: In July 1932, at Loch Lomond, Don broke the water speed record in Miss England III, recording a time of 192.81 km/h (119.81 mph).

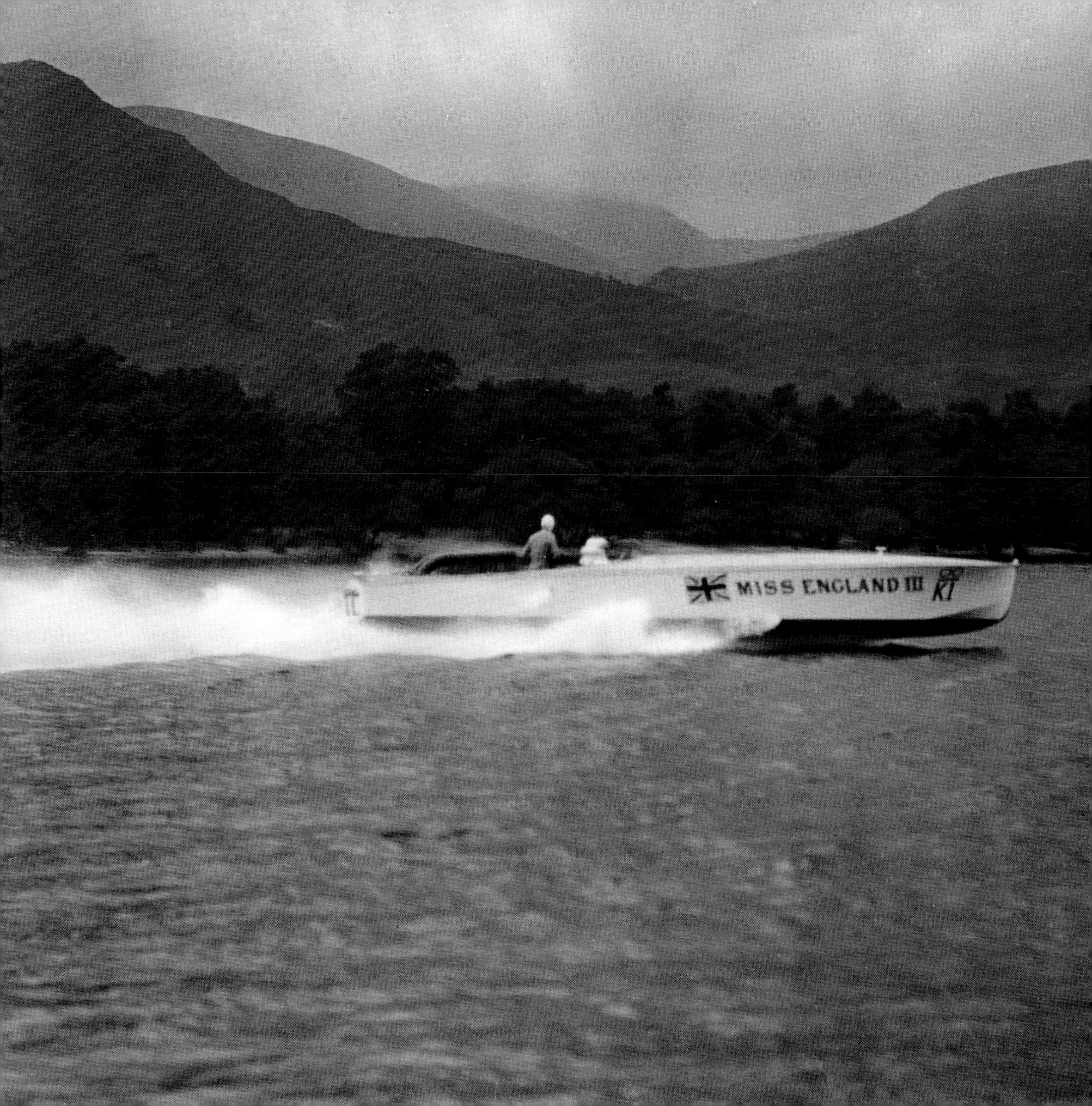
MISS ENGLAND III
K1

Malcolm Campbell
Bluebirds K3 and K4, 1937–39

IR MALCOLM CAMPBELL LIKED NOTHING BETTER THAN A CHALLENGE, ESPECIALLY WHEN IT ENTAILED BEATING AMERICA. His appetite for speed on land had finally been sated with the crowning achievement of his career, the 484.606 km/h (301.129 mph) record set at Bonneville in 1935. He then turned his attention to the 201.02 km/h (124.91 mph) water speed record, which had been in Commodore Gar Wood's hands since 1932. In 1936 Campbell commissioned Saunders-Roe to build him a 7 m (23 ft) single-step hydroplane to the design of Fred Cooper and Reid Railton. To power it he used the Rolls-Royce R engine from the Bluebird car.

Bluebird K3 (the K and the digit referred to the British system of numbering unlimited capacity craft) was ready by 1937 and for initial trials it was taken to Loch Lomond in Scotland. When conditions there proved unsuitable, Campbell transferred to Lake Maggiore on the border of Italy and Switzerland. Initially Campbell suffered the same sort of overheating problems that had plagued Kaye Don and Miss England II and III, but just as he was running out of patience Railton modified K3 and effected a temporary cure. On 1 September 1937 the speed king recorded 203.30 km/h (126.33 mph) to beat Gar Wood. The following day, in typical style, he improved that to 208.40 km/h (129.50 mph). The science of his 2000 hp, 2286 kg (5040 lb) craft had proved

convincingly superior to the brute force of Wood's 7500 hp, 8636 kg (19,040 lb) monster.

In 1938 Campbell drove K3 for the last time. On Lake Hallwil in Switzerland, he pushed the boat to 210.59 km/h (130.86 mph), fighting it all the way. It was another new record, but he knew it was as fast as it would go. What he needed was something completely new.

Railton supplied him with Bluebird K4, which utilized a new concept pioneered by Arno and Adolf Apel in America. Instead of running on a vee-shaped single step at the front, and a skid at the back, their boats ran on three points. The front step was split in two and separated by a large area of flat floor, giving much better stability and lifting the hull right to the surface of the water, reducing drag dramatically. This three-point suspension system remains the fundamental concept of record boats to the present day.

K4 was 8.2 m (27 ft) long and just over 3.3 m (11 ft) wide, and was much more advanced than K3. On 19 August 1939, on Coniston Water, Campbell achieved the least troubled record of his career, a quantum leap to 228.10 km/h (141.74 mph). The future had arrived.

After the war Campbell ushered in the jet age when he had a de Havilland Goblin turbojet engine of 2268 kg (5000 lb) thrust installed in K4, but he was now 62, his eyesight was suffering and the modified boat was a brute to drive. He died on the last day of 1948, still planning to go faster.

Top: Malcolm Campbell in his Bluebird K3 in the trials at Loch Lomond 1937.

Bottom: Bluebird shows what she can do in trials at Poole Harbour in Dorset.

Opposite: Malcolm Campbell breaks the water speed record with K3 at Lake Hallwil in Switzerland, September 1938.

John Cobb
The jet-propelled Crusader, 1952

SIR MALCOLM CAMPBELL'S BLUEBIRD K4 HAD MATED A TURBOJET ENGINE TO A SPEEDBOAT HULL FOR THE FIRST TIME, in its Coniston Slipper guise in 1947. But the first boat designed specifically to take advantage of pure jet thrust was John Cobb's elegant Crusader.

Like Campbell, Cobb turned to the water speed record after breaking the land speed record on three occasions. As he and designer Reid Railton planned the new project, Cobb still held the land record at 634.38 km/h (394.20 mph). But Campbell's record of 228.10 km/h (141.74 mph) was broken twice while Crusader was under preparation. On both occasions the same driver and craft were successful. Stanley Sayres's inappositely named Slo-Mo-Shun IV employed the three-point suspension system, but took it a step forward by using the propeller itself as the third point of support. This reduced hydrodynamic drag even further and gave a valuable boost in speed. Sayres boosted Campbell's record to 258.00 km/h (160.32 mph) on Lake Washington on 26 June 1950; on 7 July two years later, at the same venue, he increased that to 287.24 km/h (178.49 mph). These were tremendous speeds for a propeller-driven boat, but Cobb was confident that Crusader had much more to offer.

Railton and Peter du Cane, chief designer of Vosper, where Crusader was built, reversed the three-point system, so that the boat ran on a single forward point just below the jet air intakes, and two outrigged at the rear. They undertook a series of intensive tests with rocket-powered scale models, until they were sure that they had identified the optimum configuration.

Crusader was ready in July 1952, and du Cane tested it for the first time in Portsmouth Harbour. By September Cobb's team, led by his old friend and Bonneville rival, George Eyston, were camped at Loch Ness. There they fought poor weather and water conditions, and mechanical problems, but on 10 September Cobb believed he had unofficially broken the record, and nine days later he averaged 278.63 km/h (173.14 mph), equalling Slo-Mo-Shun's fastest speed on one run despite high wind. Everything was finally ready for 29 September, but after a delay awaiting the right water conditions the normally calm Cobb was angered to discover one of his support boats had moved out of position, against orders. It has been speculated that its wash was a factor in the tragedy that followed.

Cobb was travelling at massive speed, around 386 km/h (240 mph), when Crusader's front planing point collapsed and the boat nosedived into the loch. Cobb was killed instantly. Later, the official figure for his run through the mile was given as 332.95 km/h (206.89 mph).

The front plane was known to have been weakened and Cobb had agreed to keep his speed down, but the ripples from the support boat's wash may have been too much. Cobb was much loved for all his taciturn nature, and his death cast another pall over a hard year for British endeavours in the realm of speed.

John Cobb gives his record-breaking Crusader an engine check at Loch Ness. Shortly afterwards, Cobb was killed when the front of the boat collapsed at high speed.

Donald Campbell
Like father like son, 1967

I F DONALD CAMPBELL HARBOURED ANY ASPIRATIONS TO FOLLOW IN HIS FATHER'S ILLUSTRIOUS WHEELTRACKS THEY WERE NOT ENCOURAGED. Sir Malcolm once suggested that Donald was so accident-prone that he would kill himself if he tried. When Donald learned, shortly after his father's death, that American industrialist Henry Kaiser intended to beat Sir Malcolm's water speed record, he was stung into defensive action. He purchased the old Bluebird K4 hydroplane from his father's estate, and refitted the Rolls-Royce R piston engine that had been replaced by the de Havilland Goblin jet.

He was 28 years old, and his first attempts to emulate his father were fraught with mechanical difficulties. Twice he was told that he had succeeded, only for the information to prove incorrect. Then, in 1950, Stanley Sayres's success with Slo-Mo-Shun IV came as a crushing blow.

Bluebird was rebuilt as a prop-rider like Slo-Mo, by a team led by Campbell's faithful engineer and mentor, Leo Villa, who had stayed with him after Sir Malcolm's death. In 1951 they were travelling above record speed on Coniston Water when the boat struck a submerged railway sleeper and was disembowelled. They were lucky to escape unharmed. Campbell then watched John Cobb's progress with interest and was saddened when he died on Loch Ness. But by the time the Italian champion, Mario Verga, perished on Lake Iseo on 9 October 1954, Campbell was already well advanced with an all-new Bluebird powered by a Metropolitan-Vickers Beryl jet engine of 1814 kg (4000 lb) thrust.

Bluebird K7 was taken to Ullswater early in 1955, but Campbell endured many teething troubles and it was not until designers Ken and Lew Norris had made many modifications that he was ready to attack the 320 km/h (200 mph) water barrier.

On 23 July that year he overcame all his problems to achieve 325.59 km/h (202.32 mph). Later that season Bluebird sank while on test at Lake Mead in Nevada, but the craft was swiftly repaired and on 16 November Campbell increased the record to 347.93 km/h (216.20 mph).

In the Fifties, holiday magnate Sir Billy Butlin offered £5000 annually to anyone who broke the record, and each year Campbell nudged it higher: 363.10 km/h (225.63 mph) in 1956; 384.73 km/h (239.07 mph) in 1957; 400.10 km/h (248.62 mph) in 1958; and 418.98 km/h (260.35 mph) in 1959.

Then came the interlude with the Bluebird car, the accident at Utah in 1960, and qualified success at Lake Eyre in 1964. On the last day of December he became the only man ever to break land and water records in the same year when he achieved 444.69 km/h (276.33 mph) on Australia's Lake Dumbleyung.

Campbell wanted to build a supersonic car. To finance it he decided to try for 483 km/h (300 mph) on Coniston Water. On 4 January 1967 Bluebird took off at an estimated 528 km/h (328 mph) and somersaulted to destruction. The body of a man of great courage was never found.

Top: *Donald Campbell and the Bluebird.*

Bottom: *Campbell piloting the jet-propelled Bluebird through its record-breaking run at Coniston Water.*

Lee Taylor
From Hustler to Discovery, 1967 and 1980

WHEN LEE TAYLOR TURNED UP AT RICH HALLETT'S BOATYARD IN DOWNEY, CALIFORNIA, in 1963, towing a big Westinghouse J46 turbojet engine, and told Rich to build him a boat around it, Hallett and onlookers just laughed. But Taylor, a former water-ski record-holder and a racer of Hallett's smaller boats, wasn't joking.

So Hallett, a master craftsman who preferred to work without detailed plans, fashioned him a beautiful chisel-nosed speedboat around the 9977 kg (6200 lb) thrust engine. Taylor persuaded Harvey Aluminum to help with finance, and in January 1964 they took the Harvey Aluminum Hustler to Lake Havasu, where Taylor soon discovered that it did not steer properly. It was taken back to Downey for modifications. On 14 April Taylor was back at Havasu, but when the throttle stuck open after a 402 km/h (250 mph) run, he had to bail out in a hurry as Hustler headed for the shore. Ironically, Hustler was damaged less than Taylor. The coastguard helicopter that rescued him crashed on take-off, compounding his injuries, which included a crushed ankle, crushed left eye and a fractured skull. He was comatose for 18 days, and it took him as many months before he learned to walk and talk again. Initially, the only word he remembered was 'California'.

He recovered gradually, but by 1966 he was back in Hustler, looking for further support. His life fell apart as his wife left him, but he pushed on, and in June 1967 he was ready to challenge the late Donald Campbell's record of 444.69 km/h (276.33 mph). His first attempt on 30 June failed, but then he finally achieved his goal with 458.993 km/h (285.213 mph) on Lake Guntersville, Alabama.

Taylor lost Hustler in a battle with sponsor John Beaudoin, and for years struggled to finance a new boat which he called US Discovery I. A mock-up was made, but nothing more. By 1980 his persistence paid off as he was able to put the final touches to a totally new craft, US Discovery II, the world's first ever rocket-powered water record-contender.

Discovery was 12 m (40 ft) long and looked like a long piece of pipe with two sponsons outrigged at the rear end. Its hydrogen peroxide engine developed 2721 kg (6000 lb) of thrust. Taylor spoke of eventual speeds significantly faster than 800 km/h (500 mph).

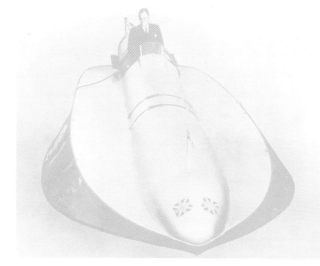

US Discovery II was taken to Walker Lake, near Hawthorn in Nevada, for its initial trials in the summer of 1980. At first it wallowed in the water like an injured duck, and at times it tried to submarine if Taylor put on too much power. But gradually he coaxed it to life, claiming to have reached 530 km/h (330 mph).

On 13 November 1980 he attacked the record on Lake Tahoe. Water conditions were poor, and the boat started to roll as it hit swells. It crashed at more than 435 km/h (270 mph) and Taylor was killed instantly. Yet again, the sport lost an abnormally brave character.

Ken Warby
The Spirit of Australia, 1978

WHEN 25-YEAR-OLD KEN WARBY SAW DONALD CAMPBELL'S BLUEBIRD SET ITS FINAL RECORD OF (276.33 MPH) ON LAKE DUMBLEYUNG, near Perth in Western Australia, it sparked off a dream. Warby had built his first boat as a 13-year-old, and by 1974 he had graduated to building his own world water speed record challenger, following the concept of Lee Taylor's Hustler. Initially he wanted to call it Spirit of Anzac, but when permission was refused he settled for Spirit of Australia.

Campbell had sportingly refused to claim the Australian water speed record, so that others who might come after him had something still to aim for, and as Warby massaged his homemade boat into shape he made periodic forays to edge that record up. He worked with only a small crew of volunteer supporters, many from the Royal Australian Air Force, winning their respect with his no-nonsense approach and his own engineering ability.

First he raised the Australian record to 267 km/h (166 mph). In 1976 he raised that to 288 km/h (179 mph). Each time he added a little bit more to the boat. Then he began working in conjunction with Professor Tom Fink of the University of Sydney, a quiet academic who had taught Campbell's designer, Ken Norris, and initially been part of the Bluebird team in 1955. Fink came up with the tailplane that tamed Spirit of Australia's handling, and helped to ensure that the bows stayed glued down to avoid a repetition of Campbell's crash.

In April 1977 Warby secured a new national record of 310 km/h (193 mph), with a one-way run of 373 km/h (232 mph), then pushed that to 345 km/h (215 mph). After fitting air scoops either side of the cockpit, to eed the Westinghouse J34 engine, he set one more national record, at 394 km/h (245 mph). Then, on 20 November 1977, he achieved his goal. His original engine had been damaged, so an elderly replacement was fitted hastily. To cut down drag Warby cut a piece off the rudder. He lifted Taylor's record by a fraction, to 463.760 km/h (288.175 mph), but it was only the beginning.

Warby received the MBE, but more important to him was the assistance from the RAAF, which completely rebuilt his engine. He knew it had been down on power, and he had a point to prove. He did so on 8 October 1978 when he increased the record by the largest margin in its history, to 511.107 km/h (317.596 mph). All in a boat built literally in his own back yard. Though some have challenged it, that record still stands.

In 1997, tiring of the lack of competition, Warby was finally readying a second version of Spirit of Australia to attack his own record. 'The plan,' he said, 'is that I will drive it first to break my old record. Then my son Peter is going to drive it and really kick up the speed!'

Ken Warby, holder of the water speed record – others have struggled to break it, but no-one strives to achieve this more than Warby himself.

Craig Arfons
'You feel every bump!', 1989

WHAT CRAIG ARFONS REALLY WANTED TO DO WAS BUILD AND DRIVE THE WORLD'S FIRST SUPERSONIC CAR. But the 39-year-old drag racer knew that would take far more money than he could find. So he decided instead to make it a two-stage project, the first stage being to break Ken Warby's water speed record of 511.107 km/h (317.596 mph).

Arfons, son of Walt Arfons and nephew of Art Arfons, lived in Sarasota, Florida, where he had befriended local boat dealer David Loebenberg. Together they went into business to produce a new challenger. Arfons started with the basic mould for a Diva drag boat hull, and modified it to suit his purposes. It was made of glass-fibre with tri-directional lay-up, and used Kevlar, the material used for F1 car chassis and bulletproof vests, for extra strength. The finished boat measured 7.6 m (25 ft) in length with a beam of 2.4 m (8 ft). It weighed only 1134 kg (2500 lb) and was powered by a General Electric J85-17 turbojet engine from a Learjet. Warby had tried an afterburner, a device that injects raw fuel into the exhaust gas stream to augment power, but had not managed to make it work properly. Arfons was confident that with 2268 kg (5000 lb) of thrust with the afterburner and his boat's extremely light weight he would be able to use drag boat techniques of very fast acceleration, rather than building up relatively gently as past record-contenders had tended to do. The drag boats could hit 362 km/h (225 mph) in a standing quarter mile.

His boat, as yet unnamed, was first tested on Florida's Lake Manatee before they switched to nearby Lake Maggiore in July 1988. Arfons estimated that he achieved around 257 km/h (160 mph). Later the local council let him use Lake Jackson in Sebring, where he claimed to have reached 402 km/h (250 mph) that August. 'I gained more respect for the water,' he said. 'Believe me, you feel every bump!'

Following successful tests at Jackson in November 1988, he scheduled an attempt on Warby's record for the weekend of 8 and 9 July 1989. The boat now had a sponsor and a name, the Rain-X Challenger. Though nervous, Arfons was keen to attack, and after runs on the Saturday he was ready for an all-out attempt on the Sunday. His run began just after seven o'clock, and Challenger began pitching up and down as it tended to. Then it began to tramp or roll from side to side as the speed increased. Suddenly the whole boat lifted off, skipped and bounced down again, and then lifted again and suddenly performed a corkscrew motion to the left. It made a low somersault and then rolled violently. Arfons was killed instantly.

The American Power Boat Association later ratified his peak speed as 603 km/h (375 mph).

Craig Arfons attempting to break Ken Warby's water speed record.

Betty Cook
Waterborne supergran, 1974–83

THE POUNDING IS ENOUGH TO BREAK ANKLES AND TO STRAIN BACKS AND NECKS. THE ENVIRONMENT IS ENOUGH TO TAX THE STRENGTH AND STAMINA OF THE TOUGHEST ATHLETES. Offshore powerboat racing is not a pursuit for the faint-hearted. This all places the achievements of the late Betty Cook, a grandmother from Newport Beach, California, into even sharper perspective.

Cook started her career late, and she was 51 years old when her first offshore race victory came in 1974 in her monohull, Mongoose. Three years later she reached the top of her world when she won the shoot-out for the Offshore World Championship in the Sam Griffith Trophy at Key West. It was arguably the finest achievement by a woman in the history of powerboat racing.

On 26 May 1978 she became the first person ever to complete the gruelling 935 km (580 mile) race from San Felipe to Lapaz, down the Gulf of California, east of the Baja Peninsula, in one day. She took 12 hr 45 min, averaging 80 km/h (50 mph) in her 8.8 m (29 ft) Scarab monohull. That season also won the Cowes–Torquay race at 124.59 km/h (77.42 mph), and again took the Offshore World Championship counter at Key West. The World Championship eluded her that year, but she won the national title. 1979 was possibly her best season, as she won the Offshore World Championship, racing her MerCruiser-powered 11.6 m (38 ft) Scarab monohull and 12 m (40 ft) Cougar catamaran under the banner of Kaama outdrives. The following year she was narrowly beaten to the accolade of first woman to achieve 160 km/h (100 mph) in an offshore craft by that other famous waterborne grandmother, Fiona, the Countess of Arran, and her new lightweight Scarab was not always as effective as its heavier predecessor in rougher water. She finished as runner-up in Class 1 to Michel Meynard's Fayva Shoes Cougar. The deciding round was at Port Philip Bay, Melbourne, where she led for all but the last few miles. What she most liked to do was to push hard and force other drivers to run their equipment to the absolute limit. In an outstanding drive she took her monohull Scarab to speeds of 145 km/h (90 mph), but was simply outpowered by Meynard's catamaran and finished a minute and a half behind. It was an honourable defeat.

The Michelob Light/New Orleans 200 at Pontchartrain in 1982 provided her with her 15th career victory at 130 km/h (81 mph), and her new Kevlar Formula catamaran left Steve Stepp two miles behind. But 1983 was a year plagued by poor reliability typified by her experience in the Long Beach to Catalina Rum Run, where Kaama led until it began to lose power and had to retire.

When she ran, Betty Cook (and throttleman John Connors) ran at the front and they ran to win. In a great career she beat the greatest names in the sport, on even terms, fair and square.

Betty Cook was 51 years old when she won her first race.

Bernie Little
No slowing down

I T IS NOT POSSIBLE TO VISIT AN AMERICAN UNLIMITED HYDROPLANE RACE WITHOUT ONE MAN'S NAME STARING YOU IN THE FACE. He is not a race driver and he is not a television commentator. Nor is he the Unlimited Commissioner. But he is the most powerful man in the sport. His name is Bernie Little, and – like another Bernie, Ecclestone in Formula One – everybody knows him.

A self-made millionaire and the owner of one of the most successful racing teams in Unlimited history, Little is one of those rare things, a legend within his lifetime. At 72, he shows no signs of slowing down.

Born in McComb, a small town in Ohio, Little learned early that the best way to the top was through sheer hard work and application. He left school early, did several paper rounds to earn money, and then discovered a lucrative opportunity awaited someone with the patience to collect lost golfballs at his local green, and to sell them on once they had been repainted.

The Second World War carried him off to the Navy at the age of 17, and one of his abiding memories of those days is being blown off the deck of his troop ship when it was hit by a suicide submarine during the Okinawa invasion. He

Bernie Little has brought new ideas of safety to the pursuit of speed on water.

spent VJ Day trawling Japan's Inland Sea, looking for magnetic mines planted by his fellow Americans. Seven of the 11 ships that carried out this hazardous duty fell foul of the mines they sought.

Little dabbled in the restaurant business and then used-car sales, before becoming a stunt pilot in a travelling air show. He discovered his niche when he started selling cars, boats and aeroplanes in St Petersburg, Florida. Then one day he saw the old four-seater Tempo Unlimited hydroplane owned by bandleader-cum-racer Guy Lombardo, and suddenly he was completely hooked. He raced it with minimal success, but then another of those chance meetings took place in 1961 when August Busch II, president of the Anheuser-Busch company which makes Budweiser beer, spotted the boat and accepted the offer of a ride. Little and Busch took 225 km/h (140 mph) turns at the wheel, and a lasting friendship and business relationship was formed.

The sport is awash with tales of Little's acumen. When the Rolls-Royce Merlin engine was the one to have, Little looked ahead and cornered the market in Rolls-Royce Griffons, but kept them up his sleeve until they were absolutely necessary. He persuaded ace Dean Chenoweth out of self-imposed retirement and he ran riot in 1979 through to 1982 in the Griffon-powered boat. But it was Chenoweth's death at Pasco that set Little on the path of safety. Through him the fully enclosed cockpit capsule became a mandatory part of today's powerboat sport. When Chenoweth died Bernie swore to do everything he could to prevent a repetition. Since then Unlimited hydroplane racing has not had a fatality.

Ron Musson
Crossing the line at maximum speed

WHEN HE WAS ASKED HOW YOU DRIVE AN UNLIMITED HYDROPLANE, SUPERSTAR PILOT BILL MUNCEY ONCE REPLIED LACONICALLY: 'CAREFULLY.'

The 11.5 m (38 ft) hydroplanes were powered, in Muncey's day, by supercharged piston aero-engines such as the Rolls-Royce Merlin or Griffon. The 290 km/h (180 mph) boats had more than 2500 hp and weighed more than 2721 kg (6000 lb). They threw up roostertails 30 m (100 ft) long and 18 m (60 ft) high which contained thousands of litres of lake water. The roostertails were so thick that other boats following too closely could literally climb up them. The men who raced them had to be something very special. Muncey was a multiple champion whose tally of 61 race victories is unlikely to be challenged, but his career ended with a fatal somersault in Acapulco in 1981 when he pushed just that bit too hard. He always maintained that, of all the drivers he raced against, Ron Musson was the greatest.

Musson had all the speed and courage that he needed, but he also had that rare ability to drive a boat to its limit in the hostile environment of a race, without overtaxing it. And he could judge the starts to perfection. Drivers would jockey for position as the hands of a giant clock moved towards the 12 o'clock position, and the knack was to cross the line at maximum speed at precisely the right moment and gain the best line for the first corner. Musson was a past master of the art.

He moved into the Unlimiteds in 1959, driving the famous Hawaii Kai III, before switching to Nitrogen Too. With that boat he took his first victories in Madison, Reno and on the Detroit River. But it was when he joined oil magnate Ole Bardahl's crack team that his career really took off. He narrowly lost the National High Points title to Muncey that season, and placed third in the 1962 season. But over the next two years Musson and the Green Dragon were uncatchable. He roared to success in both the national championship and in the prestigious Gold Cup race on the Detroit River, the Indianapolis 500 of the boat world. He won two World Championships and 16 of his 47 races.

Musson died in the President's Cup race on the Potomac River on 19 June 1966. He was driving a revolutionary Miss Bardahl which placed the engine behind the driver, in the style that has since become de rigueur. His old boat was out of commission, but he would rather race than watch, and he was killed instantly as it disintegrated at high speed.

The sport was shocked by the tragedy, then shattered by what came to be known as Black Sunday, as fellow drivers Donnie Wilson and Rex Manchester perished later that day.

Muncey was devastated. 'Those weren't recruits we lost today,' he said. 'They were the best we had.'

Ron Musson powering the Miss Bardahl – not the boat he usually raced – in which he was killed in 1966.

Bibliography

AVIATION

Chant, Christopher, *Top Gun*, London, 1992

Gunston, Bill, *The World's Greatest Airplanes: the Story of the Men who Built them and How they Came to Be*, New York, 1980

Nesbit, Roy Conyers, *Illustrated History of the RAF*, London, 1990

Parker, Steve, *Airplanes,* London, 1995

The Guinness Book of Air Facts and Feats, Enfield, 1985

EXTRAORDINARY VEHICLES

Cartmell, Robert, *The Incredible Scream Machine: A History of the Roller Coaster*, Ohio, 1987

Clew, Jeff, *Sammy Miller: The Will to Win*, Yeovil, 1976

Davies, Gordon Charles, *A Source Book of Unusual Vehicles*, London, 1975

Key, Mike, *Truck Racing: Circuit, Drag, Oval & Desert Truck Racing from America, Africa & Europe*, London, 1988

Myatt, Steven, *Quarter Mile: The Drag Racing Book for Spectators and Competitors*, London, 1982

Grand Prix Motor Racing

Boddy, William and Brian Laban, *The History of Motor Racing*, London, 1988

Collings, Timothy, *Schumacher,* London, 1994

F1 Racing, issues 1 (March 1996) to 22 (December 1997)

Frère, Paul, *Sports Car and Competition Driving*, Sparkford, 1993

Gill, Barrie, *Motor Racing: The Grand Prix Greats*, London, 1972

Hayhoe, David and David Holland, *Grand Prix Data Book*, Croydon, 1995

Higham, Peter, *The Guinness Guide to International Motor Racing*, Enfield, 1995

Hill, Damon, *Damon Hill's Grand Prix Year*, London, 1994

INDY CAR RACING

Amabile, Rick, *Inside Indy Car Racing 1991*, Fresno, 1991

Cansidine, Tim, *American Grand Prix Racing*, Osceola, 1997

Engel, Lyle Kenyon, *The World's Most Exciting Auto Race, Indianapolis 500*, New York, 1972

Ferguson, Andrew, *Team Lotus: The Indianapolis Years*, Sparkford, 1996

Sakkis, T., *Indy Racing Legends*, Osceola, 1996

LAND SPEED RECORDS

Ackroyd, John, *Just for the Record*, London, 1984

Posthumus, Cyril and David Tremayne, *Land Speed Record*, London, 1984

Scott-Simmers, Kate (comp.), *British Land Speed Records*, Slough, 1996

Tremayne, David, *The Fastest Man on Earth – The Inside Story of Richard Noble's Land Speed Record*, London, 1986

Tremayne, David, *The Land Speed Record*, London, 1991

MOTOR CYCLE RACING

Clifford, Peter, *The Art and Science of Motor Cycle Road Racing*,
　Richmond, 1985
Cutts, John & Michael Scott, *The World's Fastest Motor Cycles*, London, 1990
Heuval, Cock van de, *Pictorial History of Japanese Motorcycles*, Devon, 1997
McDiarmid, Mac, *Classic Super Bikes from around the World*, Bristol, 1996
Ryder, Julian, *World Superbike: The first ten years*, Somerset, 1997
Walker, Mick, *Hamlyn History of Motorcycles*, London, 1997
www.2wf.com – 2 Wheel Freaks, a Web Site devoted to road racing
　motor cycles

NASCAR

Fieldon, Greg, *Forty Years of Stock Car Racing*, Vol. II, *The Superspeedway Boom
　1959–1964*, Madison, 1990
Fieldon, Greg, *Forty Years of Stock Car Racing*, Volume IV, *The Modern Era
　1972–1989*, Madison, 1990
Hungness, Carl, *The 1994 Indianapolis Stock Cars Yearbook*, Madison, 1994
Hungness, Carl, *The 1995 Indianapolis Stock Cars Yearbook*, Madison, 1995
UMI Publications Ltd, *The Official NASCAR Preview and Press Guide 1997*,
　Charlotte, 1997

PRODUCTION CARS

Clarkson, Jeremy, *Jeremy Clarkson's Motorworld*, London, 1996
Heilig, John, *Mercedes Benz SL*, Yeovil, 1997
Kuah, Ian, *Dream Cars*, London, 1988
Lis, Alan, *Ferrari, the Classic Experience*, Somerset, 1991
Nixon, Chris, *Racing the Silver Arrows*, London, 1986
Porter, Philip, *Jaguar XJ220*, London, 1994
www.supercars.net – Super Cars, a Web Site featuring many of the world's
　fastest production cars

TRAINS AND RAILWAYS

Allen, Cecil J., *Titled Trains of Great Britain*, Addlestone, 1967
Connell, Stephanie, *Railways and Trains*, London, 1976
Hollingsworth, Brian, *Modern Trains*, London, 1985
Nock, O. S., *World Atlas of Railways*, Bath, 1978
Whitehouse, Patrick B., *Great Trains of the World*, London, 1975

WATER SPEED RECORDS

Campbell, Donald, *Into the Water Barrier*, London, 1955
Desmond, Kevin, *Power Boat Speed*, London, 1988
Tance, Adrian, *Fast Boats and Flying Boats*, Ensign, 1989
Tremayne, David, *Racers Apart*, London, 1991
Villa, Leo and Kevin Desmond, *The World Water Speed Record*, London, 1976

Glossary

Airscrew
Alternative term to describe a propeller as used in aircraft. When used as a propulsion method for trains, very high speeds can be attained, but at the cost of heavy fuel consumption.

Bogie
The suspension unit that connects a train to its wheels. The configuration of bogies is often used to describe a locomotive. For instance, a 4-4-2 would have a pair of four-wheel bogies and a single two-wheel bogie.

Broad-gauge
Broad-gauge refers to railway tracks wider than the standard gauge (see also *Standard gauge*).

Caboose
A car or carriage on a train that provides facilities for the crew. A train running without any other carriages is often referred to as being with 'Caboose only'.

Camshaft
In internal-combustion engines, a rotating shaft with attached irregular forms called cams. These actuate the intake and exhaust valves of the cylinders in a prescribed sequence.

Catenary system
Catenary is a term to describe the shape of a cable when suspended between supporting points. A Catenary system suspends high-tension electricity cables above a railway track to provide overhead power to trains.

Chassis
The structural frame upon which a vehicle is constructed (see also *Monocoque*).

Chicane
A narrow and often winding section of racetrack. Frequently designed as a safety feature to reduce vehicles' speeds, a chicane severely tests the skills of drivers.

Delta wings
Aeroplane wings that are triangular in shape like those of Concorde: from the Greek letter Delta.

Desmodronic valve drive
A sophisticated means of controlling opening and closing of valves in an engine, using hydraulics to provide flexible and precise timing cycles.

Drag coefficient
A mathematical expression to demonstrate how aerodynamic a vehicle's hull or body is: the lower the figure, the less drag.

G-force
The force experienced by a pilot or driver whilst accelerating/decelerating violently, measured as a multiple of the Earth's gravitational pull. For example, a force of 3 Gs is equivalent to three times the Earth's gravitational pull.

Hemispherical combustion chamber
A hemispherical chamber in which a mixture of fuel and air is combusted under pressure to provide motive power.

Hypersonic
A speed very much in excess of the speed of sound (see also *Speed of sound*). Usually used with reference to rockets and missiles.

MACH
The ratio of the speed of a moving object to the local speed of sound (see also *Speed of sound*). Mach 1 is equivalent to the speed of sound, Mach 2 is twice that speed, and so on.

Monocoque
A vehicle constructed without a chassis. All structural strength is gained from the vehicle's shell (see also *Chassis*).

Monohull
A monohull vessel has a single hull – the traditional shape for most boats. Catamarans and trimarans are types of multi-hull vessel.

Monorail system
A rail system utilizing only one rail. The train can run astride the track, being stabilized by guide wheels or gyroscopically. Or, in overhead rail versions, the gyroscopically-stabilized train is suspended by wheeled axles.

NASCAR
The National Association of Stock Car Auto Racing.

Normally aspirated
Refers to an internal combustion engine that is aspirated (provided with oxygen for the combustion process) conventionally via a carburettor.

Pantograph
A system of levers and joints that ensures constant contact between a train and its overhead electric cables (see also *Catenary system*).

Polymer-enhanced
A material with a plastic polymer additive. This can significantly increase the material's strength and durability.

Prop rider
A three-point hydroplane supported on two sponsons and the hub of the propeller.

Raked windscreen
A windscreen sloping sharply away from the direction of travel. This gives a streamlined appearance and can reduce drag.

Roll cage
A reinforced cage structure that protects the passenger compartment if the vehicle rolls on to its roof.

Slipstream
The area of reduced drag immediately behind a vehicle. Slipstream is produced as the vehicle moves through and displaces the air. It can be used by a driver following another vehicle to gain speed advantage.

Space-frame chassis
An advanced chassis design utilizing lightweight construction techniques and materials (see also *Chassis*).

Speed of sound
The speed of sound in air is considered to be 331.29 m per sec at 0°C (1,086.9 ft per sec at 32°F).

Standard gauge
Gauge is the width between the inside faces of running rails. Around three-fifths of the world's railways have the standard gauge of 1.4 m (4 ft 8.5 in). Exceptions can be found in Russia, Spain and Japan.

Steering quadrant
The mount around which the steering mechanism pivots.

Subsonic
A speed slower than the speed of sound (see also *Speed of sound.*).

Supercharged
Refers to an engine fitted with a device that increases the combustion pressure, increasing its power output.

Supersonic
A speed in excess of the speed of sound (see also *Speed of sound*).

Telemetry
Technology that allows instrument and performance measurements to be monitored remotely from a moving vehicle. Often used in space flight and record-breaking runs.

Thrust
The amount of power produced by a jet or rocket engine, which can be expressed, for example, in kilograms or pounds.

Torque
The amount of turning force supplied by an engine. When a vehicle is operated using lower gear ratios, more torque is delivered to the wheels, improving the vehicle's road-holding ability.

Traction control
A computerized sensor that controls the engine power applied to the wheels in order to improve road-holding and reduce skidding.

Traction head
The point at which a train engine's tractive effort is delivered at the wheels. A technical term for a modern locomotive (see also *Tractive effort*).

Tractive effort
The amount of force provided by a locomotive at the wheels. This is affected by rail and wheel design as well as the size of the engine. Ice, leaves and other materials on the track can reduce tractive effort.

Understeer
A term to describe the effect of a vehicle turning less than one would expect when the steering wheel is turned. This is often a feature of the car's design and not a fault.

Variable valve timing
The ability to change the timing cycle of an engine's valves. This allows the power band of the engine to be varied according to the driver's requirements.

Weight distribution
The way that a vehicle's weight is spread around its structure. Skilful design of weight distribution can significantly improve a vehicle's handling.

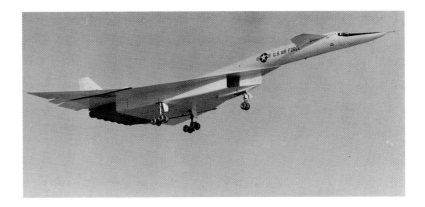

Author Biographies

Nigel Gross: Aviation
Nigel Gross has been an author for some 15 years and is also a keen collector of trivia. He has written over 30 books and contributed to numerous television shows and magazines. Surrounded by an ever-growing library, he now lives in Kent where he continues to write across a broad spectrum.

Richard Noble: Foreword
Richard Noble founded and has managed the Thrust project since 1974. Its objective has been to regain the world's land speed record for Britain. This was achieved when the Thrust 2 car reached 1019.44 km/h (633.468 mph) in 1983. This record stood for nearly fourteen years until it was broken by the ThrustSSC team in 1997 with the world's first supersonic run of 1227.952 km/h (763.035 mph) by the ThrustSSC car, driven by Andy Green.

Anthony Peacock: Extraordinary Vehicles; Indy Car Racing; Production Cars
Anthony Peacock was born in London in 1973, and studied modern languages at Queen's College, Oxford. He currently lives in London where he works for *Autosport,* Britain's bestselling motor sport magazine.

Kevin Raymond: Motorcycle Racing
Kevin Raymond has spent the last eight years working as a freelance journalist and photographer on many of the major motorcycle magazines. He has also contributed to a number of books on the subject and is currently Editor of *What Bike?* magazine.

Tim Scott: NASCAR
Tim Scott was born in Sherborne, Dorset, in 1976. He graduated in history from the University of York in July 1997. He is currently based in London where he works at *Autosport* magazine.

Jon Sutherland: Trains and Railways
Jon Sutherland has written more than 60 books over the past 10 years on a range of subjects. These include transport, sport, business education and children's adventure stories. He now lives in Suffolk.

David Tremayne: Introduction; Land Speed Records; Water Speed Records
David Tremayne is a freelance F1 motor sport journalist and a leading authority on land and water speed records. He was present at the Thrust 2 and ThrustSSC record attempts at the Black Rock Desert in Nevada, and is currently preparing for an attempt on the British propeller-driven water speed record.

Alexander von Wegner: Grand Prix Motor Racing
Alexander von Wegner studied Political Science, Modern History and Sociology at the Universities of Saarbrücken and Newcastle-upon-Tyne. In 1996 he covered various German motor racing series for the German TV sports channel DSF, and currently works for the German edition of *F1 Racing* and the German *GT Racing* magazine.

Other contributers were Frauke Lange, Stewart MacDiarmid and Ian Powling.

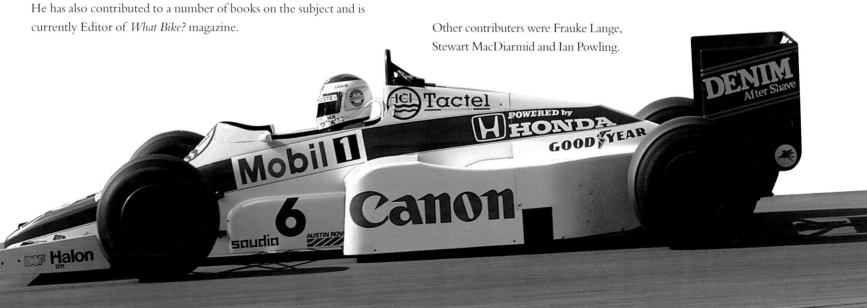

Picture Credits

Allsport UK Ltd: Mike Powell 13 (br), Tony Duffy 14, Simon Bruty 50, Simon Bruty 51, Mike Powell 52, 62, Tony Duffy 64, Tony Duffy 65, Michael Cooper 69, 71, 75 (tl), Michael Cooper 75 (tr), MSI 76 (l), Pascal Rondeau 76 (br), Pascal Rondeau 80 (tl), Mike Hewitt 82 (b), 113 (all), David Taylor 132-33, David Taylor 134 (l), David Taylor 135, David Taylor 136 (all), David Taylor 137 (all), Steve Swope 138, David Taylor 139, J. D. Cuban 140, Steve Swope 141, Andy Lyons 142, Andy Lyons 143, 187, Andy Lyons 195 (l). **Austin J. Brown/The Aviation Picture Library:** 8 (l), 13, 14, 18 (b), 22, 23, 26, 27, 28, 29, 30, 31, 32, 33, 34, 35, 38, 39, 195. **Eric Clark/BMFA:** 48, 49. **Cedar Park, Ohio:** 47. **Mirco De Cet:** 86 (l), 122, 123, 124, 125, 126 (b), 127, 129 (l), 131 (l), 152, 153, 155 (r), 156, 157, 159 (r), 160 (tl), Porsche 160 (tr&br), 161 (b). **EMPICS Sports Photo Agency:** Steve Etherington 54-55, John Marsh 68, Phil O'Brien 70, Steve Etherington 72, Steve Etherington 73, Steve Etherington 74 (l), John Marsh 74 (r), John Marsh 76, Steve Etherington 77 (all), John Marsh 78, Steve Etherington 79 (all). **Fujiyama Highland Park, Japan:** 42, 43. **Jaguar Cars:** 151. **Getty Images:** 184. **IMS Photos, Indianapolis:** 8 (r), 11 (t), 84-85, 87 (all), 88, 89 (r), 94, 95. **Italian State Railways:** 166, 168. **LAT Photographic:** 9, 12 (l), 63, 66, 80 (tr), 81 (t&b), 82 (t), 83 (tl,bl&tr), McKlein 98-99, 150 (l), 161 (t), 196 (r). **Ludvigsen Library Ltd:** 11 (b), 13 (bl), 56, 57, 58, 91, 96, 97, 100, 101 (b), 102 (all), 103, 104, 109, 110 (all), 111, 112, 154 (tr), 192 (all). **Mary Evans Picture Library:** 18 (t), 19 (r), 164 (l), 165. **Mac McDiarmid:** 114, 115, 121.

Millbrook House Limited: 162-63. **Don Morley International Sports Photo Agency:** 10, 12 (tr), 15 (l), 60, 61, 67, 106 (tl), 107 (tl), 116, 117 (all), 118, 119, 120 (all), 126 (t), 127 (t), 128, 129 (tl), 130 (tl,tr&bl), 131 (br), 193 (br), 196 (l), 197. **The Motors Hall of Fame:** 189. **Pocono Speedway:** Gregg Crisp 144, Gregg Crisp 145 (l), Ken Sherman 145 (r). **Quadrant Picture Library:** 16-17, 24, © Auto Express 44, © Auto Express 45, © Autocar 56, © Autocar 57, © Autocar 59, 101 (t), 105, © Autocar 106 (bl), 108, © Roland Brown 129 (br), © Phil Talbot 131 (tr), © Simon Everett 148, © Simon Everett 149, © Simon Everett 150 (r), © Simon Everett 154 (br), © Bob Masters 155 (l), © De Cet 158 (t), © Auto Express 158 (b), © Phil Talbot 159 (tl&bl), © Auto Express 160 (bl), © David Sparkes 172, © David Sparkes 173 (t), © Anthony R. Dalton 173 (b), © Anthony R. Dalton 174 (l), © Autocar 175, © Autocar 176-77, © Autocar 185 (t), © Autocar 186, © Autocar 193 (tl&bl). **Jonathan Reeves:** 40-41, 53. **Science and Society Picture Library:** 167. **Sporting Pictures UK Ltd:** 86 (tr), 89 (l), 90, 92. **Topham Picturepoint:** 15 (br), 19 (l), 20, 21, 25, 36, 37, 93, 106 (tr), 107 (tr&br), 130 (br), 134 (r), 146-47, 151 (b), 154 (bl), 158 (m), 164 (r), 169, 170, 171, 174 (r), 178, 179, 180, 181, 182 (all), 183, 185 (b), 188, 190 (r), 194. **David Tremayne Archive:** 190 (l), 191.

Every effort has been made to contact the copyright holders and we apologise in advance for any omissions. We would be pleased to insert the appropriate acknowledgement in any subsequent editions of this publication.

Speed **and power**

Subject Index

Index of Names

Speed **and power**